THE Kangaroo

TEXT: MICHAEL ARCHER, ASSOCIATE PROFESSOR OF ZOOLOGY,
UNIVERSITY OF NEW SOUTH WALES AND DR TIM F. FLANNERY
OF THE AUSTRALIAN MUSEUM. WITH GORDON C. GRIGG,
ASSOCIATE PROFESSOR OF BIOLOGY, UNIVERSITY OF SYDNEY.

KEVIN WELDON

THE
Kangaroo

Acknowledgments

The authors would like first to acknowledge the help of the National Geographic Society for providing the research funds (to Archer; Grant No. 2699-83) that enabled them to significantly increase understanding of the poorly-known mammals of New Guinea. This research is ongoing and it is hoped will continue for several years. Other mammal workers involved in the field-based project included Flannery, K.Aplin, P.Baverstock, M.Krogh, S.Van Dyck, H.Parnaby and P.Wilson. The support of the University of New South Wales and the Australian Museum is gratefully acknowledged. Archer was also supported by the Queensland Museum when much of the primary data were gathered. The following people helped with various aspects of the project. Ms Trina Deguara and Margaret Brennan typed many of the first drafts of the species accounts; Ms Suzanne Hand, Debbie Andrew, Jenny Taylor and Georgina Hickey helped with the compilation of much of the primary data about the Australian species of kangaroos; Ms Paula Flannery and Elizabeth Archer helped with aspects of the compilation of primary reference materials for the species accounts.

Managing Editor: Nicholas Brash
Production Manager: Gary Baulman
Production Design Development: Cecille Haycock
Administration Executive: Pamela Seaborn

Published by Weldons Pty Ltd, 43 Victoria Street, McMahons Point, NSW 2060, Australia.

First published 1985

© Copyright Weldons Pty Ltd 1985

Typeset in Australia by BudgetSet. Produced in Australia for the publisher. Printed by Dai Nippon Printing Co. Ltd, Tokyo.

National Library of Australia Cataloguing-in-Publication Data:

Archer, Michael (1945–)
The Kangaroo
ISBN 0 949708 22 4.

1. Kangaroos. 2. Marsupials – Australia. 3. Marsupials – New Guinea. I. Flannery, Tim F. (Tim Fridjof), 1956– . II. Grigg, Gordon C. (Gordon Clifford). III. Title.

559.2

Designed by John Bull, Bull's Graphics.

A Kevin Weldon production.

CAPTIONS FOR PHOTOGRAPHS PAGES 1–5

Page 1 A Western Grey Kangaroo.

Pages 2–3 Eastern Grey Kangaroos silhouetted in the moonlight of the Southern Alps.

Page 5 Male Red Kangaroos fight for supremacy.

BLACK-FOOTED ROCK WALLABY AT DAWN IN QUEENSLAND'S SELWYN RANGE.

THE WATCHFUL AGILE WALLABY.

FOREWORD

BY GERALD DURRELL

Biologically speaking, the Australian continent is one of the most fascinating and important areas of the world. The enormous range of unique creatures that inhabit it make it a treasure house from the point of view of a zoologist and a source of fascination to the layman. Where in one continent can you find such a collection of strange creatures? Something as bizarre as a Duck-billed Platypus (which always looks to me like Donald Duck in a fur coat), something as idiotically appealing as a koala or a creature so streamlined and beautifully designed as a kangaroo, the weird and enchanting beast this book is all about.

We all know that, like fauna all over the world, marsupials are under pressure and a brilliant book like this will, I hope, make everyone – not just Australians – understand the importance of these wonderful creatures and the need for their conservation.

I think most people think of kangaroos as being large, muscular animals bouncing about like over-excited young boxers and have no idea that there are many species that are tiny and delicate, almost deer-like in their graceful proportions. On my two visits to Australia, I was lucky enough to see and film a wide range of kangaroos, ranging from big, brash Red to the fluffy, rather bemused-looking Tree Kangaroo, from the Great Grey to the Pretty-face Wallaby. I found Australians' opinions on kangaroos (any kangaroos) and their right to existence varied widely. There was the sheep farmer who was so paranoid about them that if you said a word in their defence he was liable to exterminate you, and the sheep farmer (who looked like one of the more placid Old Testament prophets) who took me out on his spread and proudly showed me the various species of kangaroos happily grazing with his sheep and neither species jeopardising the other.

I sincerely hope that this book will go a long way to persuading the more rabid anti-kangaroo lobby to re-think their attitudes and to realise how important it is to protect these astonishing animals.

I remember watching and filming the birth of a Red kangaroo and it was one of the most miraculous and moving sights I have ever seen. The mother dug herself a small hole in the paddock in which she was confined and was leaning against the fence with her tail stuck out between her legs. In the beginning stages it was obvious from her restlessness that she was suffering some discomfort, which was extraordinary when you consider that the baby was only the size of an acorn.

It was, in fact, to all intents and purposes, an embryo, for it had been ejected into the world after a gestation period of only 33 days. It was blind and its hind legs, carefully crossed over each other, were powerless. Once it was out of the mother and resting on her tail, it had to start the Herculean task of climbing up into her pouch. This was really the equivalent of a blind man with both legs broken crawling through a thick forest to the top of Mount Everest, using only his arms as means of propulsion. The baby, as soon as it was born, with a funny, almost fish-like wiggle, left the mother's tail and started on this feat of mountaineering with absolutely no assistance from the mother herself. Slowly and valiantly the pulsating little pink blob struggled up through the thick fur. It took about ten minutes from the time it was born for it climb to the rim of the pouch. That a creature weighing only a gram (the weight of five or six pins) could have achieved this climb was a miracle in itself, but its task did not end there.

The pouch is approximately the size of a large handbag and into this the tiny kangaroo, no bigger than the end joint of my little finger, had to climb and search this enormous furry area in order to find its mother's teat. Once having found it he was fastened on to it, whereupon it would swell up in his mouth, thus making him adhere to it firmly. So well, indeed, that if you tried to pull the baby kangaroo from the mother's teat you would tear the soft mouth and cause bleeding. This has given rise to the idea that baby kangaroos are born on the teat, developing like a bud.

It was miraculous to watch this climb. After arriving in the world only half-formed, as it were, and then having to undertake this task for survival, I felt the baby kangaroo thoroughly deserved his life in his fur-lined, centrally heated pram with its built-in milk bar.

EASTERN GREY KANGAROOS GATHER AT THE MAINLAND'S SOUTHERN TIP: EMU FLAT ON WILSON'S PROMONTORY IN VICTORIA.

Contents

The graceful antilopine wallaroo of northern Australia.

THE GHOSTLY SILHOUETTE OF A BLACK-FOOTED ROCK WALLABY.

KANGAROOS: THE FOSSIL RECORD

VERYONE is familiar with kangaroos, those lithe, muscular hopping mammals of Australia's arid inland plains. However, this common image of the kangaroo relates almost entirely to the Red Kangaroo (*Macropus rufus*), a highly specialised relative newcomer on the Australian scene. For most of their history kangaroos have borne little resemblance to that acme of arid adaptation, the Red Kangaroo. Fifteen million years ago the largest kangaroo was only the size of a large rat, and more closely resembled a possum than the living kangaroo. Here we will trace the evolution of the kangaroos from tiny insignificant seed and insect eaters, through to the extinct giants of the Pleistocene Period, and then on to the great diversity of species that comprise most of the native large mammals of Australia today. This story involves not only changes in the kangaroos themselves, but also in the factors that initiated and guided kangaroo evolution: the changing face of the continent of Australia.

The Miocene Epoch: Humble Beginnings

Before the Miocene Epoch – which extends from 25 to five million years ago – kangaroos as we know them may not have existed. We certainly have no evidence of them in the fossil record before this time, and the oldest known kangaroo fossils represent very primitive species. Those early fossils come from ancient lake and river deposits in South Australia which are thought to have formed during the middle of the Miocene Epoch, about 15 million years ago. However, most of us would probably not recognise these animals as kangaroos, and from the isolated fossil teeth and foot bones that remain we can deduce that the largest of the Middle Miocene kangaroos would have weighed about 500 g; they probably did not hop, and certainly did not eat grass – for there was no grass in the area where they lived. Their fossilised remains are found in what today are sands and clays exposed on the sides of salt pans in the most arid areas of South Australia. Fifteen million years ago, when these animals lived and breathed, the area was covered in a vast rainforest intersected by huge slow-flowing rivers and expansive lakes. Freshwater dolphins, flamingoes and crocodiles shared the waters, while the forests were inhabited by many kinds of marsupials. The largest had koala-like teeth, and were about the size of large pigs. This type of giant marsupial died out, leaving no descendants. In the trees were found ringtail possums and koalas, different from but similar to those living today, as well as other more unusual and completely extinct kinds of marsupials.

The remains of the tiny kangaroos that shared this habitat give us many clues about their lifestyles. We can deduce from the shape of their fossilised foot bones that they had abandoned the arboreal existence of their ancestors to become ground dwellers, and that at this stage in their evolution they progressed on all fours – without hopping. Perhaps they had come down from the trees for the same sort of reasons that led our own ancestors to abandon their lofty homes: to exploit new food resources or to escape competition from other species. The fossilised teeth of these earliest kangaroos are delicate in structure and differ greatly from the robust high-crowned teeth of the modern Red Kangaroos, for example, which are developed to eat grasses. The teeth of the first kangaroos appear to be adapted to an omnivorous diet of worms, insects, fruits and even small vertebrates. Much the same kinds of foods that are eaten by some small omnivorous possums and kangaroos, such as the brushtail possums and rat-kangaroos living today.

The isolated fossilised teeth and foot bones of the earliest known kangaroos are so fragmentary that palaeontologists cannot tell whether the animals that left them belonged to one of the two great families of kangaroos: the Potoroidae (rat-kangaroos) and Macropodidae (kangaroos and wallabies), or whether they belonged to a more primitive group that gave rise to them. These two families represent fundamentally different kinds of kangaroos: the potoroids are generally small omnivorous species, many of which eat a great deal of fungi, whereas the macropodids are almost all larger species adapted to eating leaves and grasses. Fossils from a little later in the Miocene Epoch do, however, indicate the presence of these two families.

The Middle Miocene potoroids and macropodids might have weighed a kilogram or two which is a little larger than the earlier kinds of kangaroos but much smaller than most living species. At the time these kangaroos lived, little had changed in central Australia. The great rainforests still persisted, inhabited by many bizarre and now extinct animals such as giant horned turtles and

AN ARTIST'S IMPRESSION OF ONE OF THE EARLIEST KANGAROOS.

short-faced possums (ektopodontids). Between this time and eight million years ago the kangaroos gradually increased in size. Curiously, as the kangaroos grew larger, other kinds of herbivores that were similar in size became extinct. By the time kangaroos as large as 5 kg in weight had evolved, the strange herbivores with koala-like teeth had become extinct. By the time kangaroos weighing 60 kg had appeared, the smaller diprotodontids (wombat-like browsing herbivores) had also vanished, and by the end of the Pleistocene (10,000 years ago), when there were some very large kangaroos, all but the largest (bull-sized) diprotodontids had disappeared. This circumstantial evidence suggests that as the kangaroos evolved they displaced less well-adapted herbivores of a similar size, perhaps because of competition for food resources. Another curious phenomenon of this period was the development among the small, omnivorous potoroids (rat-kangaroos) of a group of species that had teeth strikingly similar to those of macropodids. These species presumably browsed from bushes in much the same way as some wallabies do today, but they, in turn, became extinct as the macropodids increased in number and variety. Presumably they were unable to compete for the limited food resources with the larger, better adapted macropodids.

Although Australia had slowly been drifting northwards (after breaking away from Antarctica about 45 million years ago), the climate and many habitats remained relatively stable throughout the Middle Miocene Epoch. But eight million years ago great changes were underway. The centre of the continent had begun to dry out and the rainforests that once covered it gradually retracted to the continental margins, where, to a limited extent, they still exist today.

The animals that inhabited those shrinking rainforests had to adapt to the drier conditions – or face extinction. The kangaroos were one of the most successful groups of marsupials to adapt to life in the now more open forests and grassy plains. Many types of tiny rainforest-living kangaroos doubtless lived on but they, together with their habitat, became extinct in most areas and survived only in favoured locations around the edge of the continent. There were many kangaroo species by this time, some perhaps as heavy as 60 kg, which is about as large as the largest living kangaroos. Fossils from the later part of the Miocene and Early Pliocene indicate that the rat-kangaroos had developed the major lineages that are seen today: bettongs, potoroos and musky rat-kangaroos. Fossils of the earliest ancestors of a group of now extinct gigantic rat-kangaroos also survive from this period. The kangaroos and wallabies, however, do not appear to have differentiated to such a great extent by this time. Only relatives of the New Guinea forest wallabies among modern forms seem to have been present.

The foot bones of the larger species indicate that they hopped, unlike their smaller ancestors, which may have progressed on all four limbs using a leaping or bounding action. Hopping is a very efficient means of locomotion for kangaroos in more open areas. Even today, some of the smaller kangaroos living in denser habitats tend to bound rather than hop. However, a final barrier had yet to be crossed. None of the Late Miocene kangaroos had teeth adapted to eating grass. Almost all had the low-crowned teeth typical of those forms called browsers that eat leaves and herbs. Thus while many kangaroos eight million years ago probably lived in open areas, it is likely they could not take advantage of grass which was the most abundant source of food in that habitat.

There is a large gap in our knowledge of kangaroo evolution between the end of the Miocene and the beginning of the Pliocene Epochs. It was during this time that the kangaroos first evolved teeth suitable for grass-eating, and the first forms that would have been referrable to many modern genera evolved. Fossils dating from this time would doubtless reveal much about the relationships of the living kangaroos and also much about how kangaroos first adapted to grass-eating. These latest Miocene fossils must be lying in the ground somewhere in Australia, awaiting the sharp eye of an amateur naturalist or scientist to bring them to light.

THE PLIOCENE: DAWN OF THE MODERN FAUNA

By the beginning of the Pliocene Epoch (which extends from five to two million years ago) Australia more closely resembled the country that we know today. Open woodland and savannah (but not vast deserts) occupied most of central Australia, although on the east coast rainforest was still widespread and more extensive than it is at present. While Middle Miocene species were only distantly related to living forms, some of the early Pliocene species resembled modern grey kangaroos, rock wallabies and pademelons as well as several other still living kinds. While not the same species, in the flesh they would probably be recognisable as very close relatives if they could be seen today.

The largest of the Early Pliocene kangaroos were the ancestors of the grey kangaroos. They probably weighed about half as much again (some 150 kg) as their living relatives. Also by this time the rat-kangaroos, which previously made up a large percentage of the kangaroo species, had sunk into relative obscurity, eclipsed in importance by the vast increase in the number of species of kangaroos and wallabies, a large proportion of which is still with us today.

Because of the extensive rainforests along the east coat of Australia, types currently confined to New Guinea and the Atherton Tablelands area of north Queensland then extended as far south as Victoria. A fossil-bearing soil, which is overlain by a 4.5 million year old lava flow near Hamilton in southwestern Victoria, contains the remains of Dorcopsis wallabies (currently found only in New Guinea) and tree kangaroos, both of which are similar to but smaller than living species. This probably does not indicate a warmer climate at the time but just wetter conditions and more extensive rainforests. It is in Pliocene sediments that we also find the earliest remains of sthenurine (short-faced) kangaroos, a bizarre group of macropodids that flourished in the following Pleistocene Epoch, but became almost completely extinct before Europeans arrived in Australia. The Pliocene Epoch is a time of transition between the ancient Miocene faunas and those of modern Australia.

Few groups of kangaroos are restricted only to the Pliocene, but one that flourished during this period, and became extinct shortly after is the genus *Troposodon*. They were mainly browsing kangaroos that varied from about 20 to 120 kg. Most of the smaller species evolved in the Early Pliocene, the larger forms apparently developing later. *Troposodon* species were sthenurine kangaroos whose only living relative is the tiny Banded Hare Wallaby (*Lagostrophus fasciatus*), now found only on Bernier and Dorre Islands off Western Australia. While we do not know what the colour patterns of most sthenurines were, it has been suggested that because the Banded Hare Wallaby has a banded rump, some *Troposodon* species also sported stripes.

AN ARTIST'S IMPRESSION OF A SPECIES OF *PROPLEOPUS* AND *TROPOSODON* (WITH A BANDED COAT).

Perhaps some were even Australia's colour equivalents of Africa's zebras and Okapi.

Another remarkable group of sthenurine kangaroos that first appeared in the Early Pliocene but did not diversify until some three million years later – in the Pleistocene Epoch – is the genus *Simosthenurus*. These strange kangaroos probably arose from *Troposodon*-like ancestors that underwent some highly unusual changes. Their faces became foreshortened and deep and the nasal region of some became greatly expanded. The number of toes decreased, leaving only a single powerful toe, the fourth (the second smallest on our feet). Two of the fingers on each hand became much longer than the rest. Most of the species of *Simosthenurus* were probably no larger than Red Kangaroos, but their proportions were very different. Their large marsupial bones (which attach to the pelvis) indicate that they had enormous guts in which to ferment vegetable matter. Their teeth were not designed for grass-eating, leaving us to deduce that they probably fed on herbs and bushes. These unusual adaptations may have allowed them to become particularly efficient browsers, and fill the same niche as deer in other parts of the world. Only a few species of *Simosthenurus* are known from the Pliocene, but in the following epoch (the Pleistocene) they became very abundant. Their more primitive relatives (the species of *Troposodon*) became extinct just as the *Simosthenurus* species were becoming dominant. This may have been the result of competition for food and/or space between the species of *Simosthenurus* and the less specialised species of *Troposodon*.

THE PLEISTOCENE EPOCH: RISE AND FALL OF THE GIANTS.

The Pleistocene Epoch (from two million to 10,000 years ago) was a time of great change. Extreme fluctuations in climate saw the growth and retreat of the great ice sheets at the Earth's poles, a phenomenon that was repeated many times. Sea level fell as water was locked away in the polar ice, and then rose again as the ice melted. Faunal interchange took place between many islands as they were united with the mainland continents, and when the islands were re-formed by rising sea levels the isolated animals evolved into new kinds. As the ice crept down from the poles, temperatures and rainfall decreased everywhere. During the heights of the glacial periods much of central

Australia was over-run by windblown dunefields with very little vegetation cover to hold the sand dunes in place. Rainforests became even further restricted to tiny pockets in the most favoured habitats, and the higher mountains became covered by snowfields and glaciers.

During this time many new kinds of kangaroos developed in response to the newly-developed and widespread arid conditions. Truly arid-adapted species such as hare wallabies, nail-tailed wallabies, the Desert Rat-kangaroo (*Caloprymnus campestris*) and the Red Kangaroo (*Macropus rufus*) appear for the first time in the fossil record of the Pleistocene. In addition to these species, the Pleistocene fossil record contains evidence of many kinds of bizarre giant kangaroo species that are now extinct. Some of these may have developed in response to the extremely arid conditions that predominated in the Pleistocene. Perhaps the most unusual of the groups of giant kangaroos of this time, and one that is restricted to the Pleistocene, is the genus *Procoptodon*. This genus includes the largest kangaroo ever to have existed: *Procoptodon goliah*. It is difficult to estimate the weight of such an unusually proportioned kangaroo as *Procoptodon goliah*, but some individuals probably weighed as much as 200–300 kg. The *Procoptodon* species appear to have developed from forms similar to the species of *Simosthenurus*. The two groups differ primarily in their teeth, which in the species of *Procoptodon* seem to be well-adapted to cope with a diet made up primarily of grasses. The species of *Procoptodon* were restricted to eastern Ausralia where they seem to have inhabited the more arid areas. Their abundant fossilised remains have been found in old sand-dunes in the Menindee region of western New South Wales as well as in many other places.

The short faces, forward directed eyes and deep jaws of the species of *Procoptodon* give them a slightly human appearance above the neck, but below this point they are pure kangaroo. The huge legs ended in a single toe, much as in horses where a single hoof is present. This one-toed condition may denote a similar function in both the species of *Procoptodon* and horses – the ability to progress rapidly in a single direction, an adaptation useful to plains-dwelling animals with little cover to retreat to if threatened. The arms of *Procoptodon* were as unusual as the feet. They were very long and mobile. Each hand had two very long fingers with thin, straight claws and three much shorter fingers. The two long claws may have acted as grappling hooks to bring foliage within reach. Although foliage may not have been their food of choice (because their teeth are primarily adapted to eating grass) foliage may have been eaten in times of drought when grass was sparse.

During the Pleistocene, one group of rat-kangaroos (genus *Propleopus*) also reached extraordinary size. The largest living rat-kangaroo, the Rufous Rat-kangaroo (*Aepyprymnus rufescens*) only reaches 3–4 kg in weight, but the extinct species of *Propleopus* probably weighed over 70 kg. Apart from their huge size, their other highly unusual feature is that they may have been carnivorous. Although a carnivorous kangaroo may seem strange, it is not quite so unusual when one considers the diets of some of the living rat-kangaroos. The Musky Rat-kangaroo (*Hypsiprymnodon moschatus*), for example, eats insects, while the Burrowing Bettong (*Bettongia lesueur*) has even been known to scavenge from the carcasses of sheep. The species of *Propleopus* all possessed large shearing premolars and very stout, sharp lower incisors. One species from northern Queensland even had a reduced grinding molar area and may have been more specialised as a carnivore than the others. Perhaps further discoveries of the skeleton of these enigmatic kangaroos, which at present are known only from a few fossilised jaws, skull fragments and some limb bones, will reveal more about their lifestyle.

Most of the early kangaroo fossils are very fragmentary, rarely consisting of more than parts of the skull. However, there are some remarkably well-preserved Pleistocene kangaroo fossils. The most complete have been found in clays overlying the brown coal seams mined at Morwell in Victoria. These clays were deposited in deep lakes formed when coal seams exposed on the surface spontaneously ignited. Little oxygen could reach the bottom of these lakes. As a result, the bodies of animals that drowned in the lake sank to the bottom and probably rotted extremely slowly. So far, the remains of three species of Morwell kangaroos have been found. Although two million years old, surprisingly the grass in the stomach area is still green. Impressions of skin, nails and mats of fur have been found, and some skeletons even have the remains of tiny joeys preserved in the region of the pouch. Extraordinary fossils such as these are rare finds, but they tell us a great deal more about once-living kangaroos than fossilised bones alone.

AN ARTIST'S IMPRESSION OF THE LARGEST KANGAROO THAT EVER LIVED – *PROCOPTODON GOLIAH*.

The last part of the Pleistocene Epoch, about 10–20,000 years ago, saw the extinction of almost all the large animals of Australia. Similar extinctions occurred on other continents. Only Africa and Asia seem to have retained their vast herds of large herbivores and predators. In Australia, the largest of the marsupials to survive, the Red Kangaroo, weighs only as much as a man. What's more, many species smaller than the Red Kangaroo also seem to have become extinct, and many of the large species that did not become extinct at this time shrank in size. Among the species whose relatives were gigantic a mere 20,000 years ago are the Western and Eastern Grey Kangaroos (*Macropus fuliginosus* and *M. giganteus*, whose ancestors probably weighed twice as much as their living descendants), and the Agile Wallaby (*Macropus agilis*). The precise causes of these extinctions and size reductions are still unknown. However, two competing theories are often put forward. One argues that when Pleistocene Man reached continents such as Australia and the Americas where species of our genus (*Homo*) did not previously exist, the indigenous large mammals could not cope with the new and efficient carnivore: as a result they were hunted into extinction. A second theory suggests that climatic change brought about the downfall of the giants. In favour of the first theory, there is a marked coincidence in time between the arrival of man on various landmasses and the extinction of the giant animals of those areas. Man arrived in Australia at least 30,000 years ago, which coincides with the beginning of the extinction of the large mammals. Palaeoindians seem to have reached the Americas 10–11,000 years ago and the extinction of most of America's large fauna dates from this time. The Maoris reached New Zealand only about 1,000 years ago, and by 500 years ago nearly all the Moas were extinct. This circumstantial evidence seems to support the idea that the hand of man rather than climatic change was involved in the last mass extinction of the world's large animals.

Between 10,000 and 200 years ago little seems to have happened to kangaroos, apart from range contractions for some species. Only a single species, Christensen's Pademelon (*Thylogale christenseni*) from mountainous New Guinea, has possibly become extinct during this time. However, the arrival of Europeans once again initiated a phase of rapid extinction of the kangaroos, but this time the extinctions

THE KANGAROO...AN INTEGRAL PART OF THE DREAMTIME.

NEW GUINEA LANDSCAPE.

appear to have affected mainly the smaller species. Among species to disappear in the last 100 years are the Toolache Wallaby (*Macropus greyi*), which was blown into oblivion by hunters in South Australia, the Eastern Hare Wallaby (*Lagorchestes leporides*) and the Crescent Nailtail Wallaby (*Onychogalea lunata*). However, the outlook is not all bleak. Due to accidental or deliberate introductions by man some species of wallaby have extended their ranges into New Zealand, Hawaii, Great Britain and Germany.

NEW GUINEA: THE GREAT REFUGE

Most of the above concerns Australia and its kangaroo fauna. The great island of New Guinea has had a very different but complementary history to its southern neighbour. Its 15 currently recognised living kangaroo species comprise 25 per cent of the total number of the living species of kangaroos. Of these, only two species are shared with Australia. New Guinea was also home to at least six now extinct gigantic kangaroo species.

At the time that the first kangaroos were coming down from the trees in central Australia, the northern parts of New Guinea did not exist. This is because this emergent landmass was the result of the collision about 15 million years ago of the continental part of the Australian plate with that of its northern neighbours. New Guinea can be thought of as the "bow wave" or northern "bumper" of Australia, which had been drifting northwards ever since it severed contact with Antarctica some 45 million years ago. Most of northern New Guinea was created when northern Australia finally collided with the Asian plates about 15 million years ago, but the southern part existed before this. The great mountain chain of central New Guinea was thrust up out of the sea as a result of this collision. It was perhaps partially as a result of this mountainous erection that less of the moisture-laden winds from the north reached central Australia. This mountain range may therefore have contributed to the drying out of Australia. As the rainforests of central Australia began to disappear, and with them the older types of central Australian mammals, almost miraculously a tiny fragment of the flora and fauna was preserved by being lifted up into the cool, cloudy, higher altitudes on the tips of New Guinea's emerging mountains.

Thus, although the plants and animals have slowly continued to change, the forests of New Guinea's mountains are in some ways a "living museum" that preserves a tiny bit of the fauna that existed in central Australia 7–10 million years ago. Only a few of the older kinds of kangaroos, however, survived in this haven. Among them were the dorcopsis wallabies, the pademelons, the tree-kangaroos and the now extinct large species of *Protemnodon*. Two species of the genus *Protemnodon* appear to have survived until around 14,000 years ago, because their fossilised remains have been found in archaeological sites in the highlands of New Guinea. The larger of the two species was probably about the size of a Red Kangaroo, and if it was similar to the better-known species of this genus which occurred in Australia, it probably possessed a long neck, very short feet and short hindlimbs, suggesting that the species of *Protemnodon* may have been slow-moving and have reached into bushes to feed. Both of the New Guinean species probably browsed on rainforest plants.

Along with the remains of these Pleistocene New Guinean kangaroos have been found the fossilised teeth and bones of a large extinct tree-kangaroo. This animal was about 10 percent larger than the largest living tree-kangaroo, Doria's Tree-kangaroo (*Dendrolagus dorianus*). These large extinct kangaroos from New Guinea, which were only named as recently as 1983, were the first extinct Pleistocene marsupials to be described from the island. In contrast, the first extinct Pleistocene marsupials from Australia were described as early as 1838. Because much of the fauna of New Guinea is so poorly known, we can look forward, hopefully in the future, to significant increases in knowledge about the living as well as extinct kangaroos of this little-explored region of Australasia.

THE KANGAROO IN THE WILD

KANGAROOS are such a diverse group that they fill a much broader ecological role than any other family or superfamily of large mammals elsewhere in the world. Perhaps their closest equivalents in the northern hemisphere are deer, cattle and sheep. However, no deer, cattle or sheep live in the treetops in rainforests, nor do they excavate complex and deep burrow systems as do some kangaroos. Among the 62 living species of kangaroos are seen many striking adaptations. Although some are paralleled in other groups of animals, others are unique. Surely the most striking feature of kangaroos is their style of locomotion for as far as we know, they are the only large mammals that hop or have ever hopped. Physiologists have shown that hopping is not as efficient as walking or running at low speeds and, indeed, kangaroos progress with a pentapedal gait, using the tail and all four limbs when moving very slowly. However, at relatively high speeds (above 17 km/h) hopping proves more efficient than running, and at these speeds a hopping Red Kangaroo requires less energy than an equivalent-sized herbivore when running. Thus hopping is clearly a great advantage to the large plains-dwelling kangaroos that often need to flee from predators or to travel long distances in search of food.

The question still remains, though, as to why kangaroos alone among large mammals have evolved this mode of progression? Perhaps they were "preadapted" to such a development. That is, maybe the structure of their ancestors made it easier for them to develop such a gait rather than to restructure their form to be able to run. But why are there no large placental mammals that hop? Could it be that placental mammals (such as ourselves) need a relatively flexible pelvis to give birth to large young and such a pelvis could not take the mechanical strain of hopping, whereas kangaroos give birth to tiny, immature young and do not need such a flexible pelvis. Whatever the reason, the means of locomotion of kangaroos is one of their most striking features and is a highly successful adaptation.

Most people realise that the majority of kangaroos eat grass and leaves. However, few know that the kangaroo itself is incapable of releasing much of the nutritive value of this food. Like sheep and cattle, the stomach of kangaroos contains many millions of specialised micro-organisms. These tiny bacteria and single-celled protistans digest the cellulose of the grass and leaves, releasing the nutrients trapped inside the plant cells which are excreted by the micro-organisms into the kangaroo's stomach. The kangaroos are then able to digest these waste products. This strange case of symbiosis (or mutual help) between large herbivores and micro-organisms developed quite independently in both the placental ruminants (e.g., cattle and sheep) and the kangaroos, and was probably developed independently in the two major kangaroo lineages, once in the rat-kangaroos (the potoroids) and once in the kangaroos and wallabies (the macropodids). We know this because the most primitive species of the potoroids lacks a specially modified stomach to hold its cellulose-eating micro-organisms, and the stomachs of the other potoroids and macropodids are specialised in different ways. The front part of the stomach in the potoroids is developed into a large sack-like structure to hold the micro-organisms, whereas in the macropodids the middle part of the stomach is developed into a long tube to hold the micro-organisms. In some species, such as the Euro, the stomach can accommodate up to one eighth of the weight of the body in food. This species needs such a large stomach because its fodder (such as spinifex) is so poor in nutrition that it needs to eat such large quantities and hold it in the stomach for a long time to allow the micro-organisms to break down the cellulose properly.

With the exception of the Musky Rat-kangaroo, all kangaroo species usually give birth to a single young at a time. The Musky Rat-kangaroo is more like many kinds of possums in that it often has twins. The young of many species take two years to develop from conception to full independence, indicating a very slow reproductive rate for the kangaroos, which would be a great disadvantage as far as survival of the species is concerned. However, many species of kangaroos have found ways of getting around this problem. Perhaps the most spectacular solution is a system called embryonic diapause. The species that have developed this system have the ability to arrest the development of the embryo at a very early point, known as the blastocyst stage, and to re-initiate embryonic growth at a later date. As soon as a young is born, the mother becomes pregnant again; but this embryo only develops to the blastocyst stage. The signal for recommencement of development seems to be the less frequent suckling by the older young. This happens when

A TROPICAL GIANT. THE ANTILOPINE WALLAROO IS THE LARGEST KANGAROO OF THE TOP END.

the older joey is eating grass as well as milk. The embryo undergoes rapid development and is born soon after. At this time the mother has the quite remarkable ability to produce two kinds of milk: one from the teat that the newborn selects, and one from the teat used by the older joey.

During short drought periods, Red Kangaroos also have a special mechanism to ensure that a birth will take place as soon as the drought breaks. The mother remains continuously pregnant, and each joey develops to about two months of age in the pouch, at which stage it weakens because of lack of nutrition due to the drought, and sucks less vigorously when dying. The reduced suckling stimulates the embryo in the womb to recommence its development. When it is born the first baby is dead and the second takes its place. This cycle is repeated again and again until the drought breaks, at which time there is a young joey waiting to take immediate advantage of the good season.

Kangaroos living in dry areas have evolved some remarkable ways of coping with a shortage of water. The Tammar Wallaby is unusual among large mammals in that it can drink seawater, and at times it gets most of its moisture from this source. The Euro and Red Kangaroo can get by with very little water and the former, given the right conditions, may be able to do without water for a considerable time.

The adaptations of the living kangaroos vary according to where the species live. To understand them better we shall begin by looking at the most ancient of kangaroo types, the rainforest-dwellers, and end by examining those newest and most adaptable of kangaroos, the desert-dwellers.

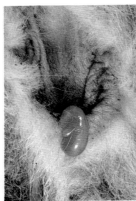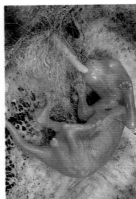

THE INCREDIBLE BEGINNINGS OF MARSUPIAL LIFE. ABOUT THE SIZE OF A BEAN, THE NEWBORN KANGAROO CLIMBS LABORIOUSLY TO ITS MOTHER'S POUCH. THERE IT FASTENS ON TO A NIPPLE AND GROWS RAPIDLY. WHEN IT HAS FUR IT HAS A "SECOND BIRTH", EMERGING FROM THE POUCH FOR THE FIRST TIME.

The Kangaroos of the Rainforest

The rainforest represents one of Australia's oldest terrestrial habitats. Because of climatic changes today it only survives in a few favoured locations. The kangaroos of the rainforest also represent very old generic types, many of which have a history going back five million years or more.

Only a single species of rat-kangaroo inhabits the rainforest: the Musky Rat-kangaroo. It is unique in a number of ways. Weighing only 500 gm, it is the smallest living kangaroo. It also retains many primitive features. It is an omnivore, eating insects and seeds and, rather peculiarly, has a grasping great toe and grooved pads on the feet. These features are seen in possums and are clearly adaptations to life in the trees. Because the Musky Rat-kangaroo lives on the ground, however, these features are probably little-used relics, reminders of the lifestyle of the ancestral kangaroos that are retained in just this one living species. The Musky Rat-kangaroo is also unusual in that it does not hop. Rather it bounds along on all fours. As a consequence, its arms and legs are similar in length — as in possums — whereas the hindlimbs are disproportionately long in the hopping kangaroos.

The Musky Rat-kangaroo is found in the Atherton Tablelands area of north Queensland but, peculiarly, is not found in New Guinea. Many other mammal species of the Atherton rainforests have close relatives or members of their own species in New Guinea.

The New Guinea dorcopsis wallabies (of the genera *Dorcopsis* and *Dorcopsulus*) and the pademelons of Australia and New Guinea are the only other terrestrial kangaroos one is likely to meet in a rainforest. Unfortunately it is still uncertain how many kinds of these animals exist in New Guinea. In Australia there are three kinds of pademelon: the Tasmanian, Red-necked and Red-legged Pademelons. Many pademelons come to the edge of the rainforest to feed at night but the New Guinea dorcopsis wallabies seem to feed inside the rainforest. The New Guinea dorcopsis wallabies display one highly unusual feature; when they are resting, most of the tail is held in a high arc with only its tip coming into contact with the ground. The reason for this bizarre adaptation is not known but it has been suggested that this may be an anti-leech device, the bulk of the tail being held so far off the ground that leeches cannot reach it!

AUSTRALIA'S BEAUTIFUL BUT DIMINISHING RAINFOREST, HOME TO MANY KANGAROO SPECIES.

It is notable that the underside of the tails of their less fortunate neighbours, the pademelons, which lack this adaptation, can become leech-infested.

Surely the most striking of all the rainforest-inhabiting kangaroos are the tree-kangaroos. Of the seven currently recognised living species of tree-kangaroo, five are found only in New Guinea. The two species found in north-eastern Queensland are the least specialised to an arboreal existence of all tree-kangaroos. There is no doubt that the tree-kangaroos arose from ground-dwelling wallabies. If they had arisen from arboreal ancestors we would expect them to have prehensile tails and grasping feet similar to those of possums and the Musky Rat-kangaroo. Instead, the ancestors of the tree-kangaroos lost these features presumably because they were adapted to life on the ground. The tree-kangaroos have had to re-adapt their distinctly unsuitable feet and tail to life in the treetops and partly as a consequence are clumsy climbers. It is rather ironic that the ancestors of all the kangaroos were well-adapted to life in the treetops but the ancestral kangaroos became so well-adapted to life on the ground that the only tree-dwelling kangaroos alive today seem relatively poorly adapted to an arboreal existence.

Although clumsy, tree-kangaroos can make great leaps of up to 18m from the treetops to the ground when alarmed. The larger species, such as Doria's Tree-kangaroo, are extremely powerful animals and New Guinean hunters report that when attacked by dogs, Doria's Tree-kangaroo can crush the snout of its tormentor in one hand. The scars on the body of many hunting dogs are a testimony to its very long and sharp claws. In some areas of New Guinea it has even been reported that tree-kangaroos have come out the victor in a struggle with a man and have driven off hunters! Some species, such as Goodfellow's Tree-kangaroo are among the most beautiful of kangaroos. However, their striking colour pattern makes them difficult to detect in their treetop homes.

The kangaroos of the rainforest have to face several difficulties not encountered in other habitats, and the various species have overcome these problems in different ways. Perhaps the greatest difficulty is that of obtaining sufficient food. In the rainforest, almost all the food is up in the treetops; and the rainforest floor is dark with few edible plants. Most pademelons find their food on the edges of

PERHAPS THE MOST UNLIKELY MARSUPIALS ARE THE TREE-KANGAROOS,
SEEKING FOOD AND REFUGE IN THE RAINFOREST CANOPY.

the rainforests, where more light reaches and plants such as grasses, bushes and herbs can grow. The tree-kangaroos, however, have simply followed their food resource into the treetops. The New Guinea dorcopsis wallabies are so poorly known that their diet and habits remain mysteries. However, they do not appear to leave the rainforest for long periods of time, nor to climb trees. The Musky Rat-kangaroo is not as affected by this problem as its larger relatives, primarily because it is small and eats insects and fallen fruit, both of which are abundant on the rainforest floor. Biting pests are a further problem for the rainforest dwellers, and we have seen how the New Guinea dorcopsis wallabies may deal with their tormentors. Tree-kangaroos generally have dense coats that may help to keep biting pests at bay.

THE KANGAROOS OF THE OPEN FORESTS, WOODLAND AND SCRUB.

Australia's woodlands and scrubs are home to the greatest diversity of kangaroos. In part, this is because these environments encompass a great diversity of habitats, from tall wet sclerophyll forest through to heath and brigalow scrub. It is in these diverse habitats that most species of bettongs, kangaroos, euros, scrub wallabies, nailtail wallabies, the Quokka and rock-wallabies are found. In some areas where many forest types are found side by side, such as northeastern New South Wales, ten or eleven species of kangaroos and wallabies can occur together, ranging in size from the Long-nosed Potoroo at about 1 kg in weight to the Eastern Grey Kangaroo which can weigh over 80 kg. This great variety of species all utilise slightly different food resources and protective cover.

The rock-wallabies and euros are nearly always found in rocky areas; the euros usually on the less steep slopes and the rock-wallabies among the pinnacles and very rough areas. Rock-wallabies are such good climbers that they have even been seen climbing trees. Species of both of these groups rest in caves during the day, where temperatures and humidity are more favourable, and come out to feed at night. These species occupy a wide variety of rocky habitats. Some rock-wallabies are found in rainforests but most live in either woodland or desert areas. Even in the desert, the rocky areas favoured by them have more diverse plant growth than the surrounding arid plains.

QUOKKAS: THE PRIMITIVE SCRUB DWELLERS OF SOUTHWESTERN WESTERN AUSTRALIA.

The tall wet sclerophyll forests of southeastern Australia harbour very few species of kangaroo. However, the Long-footed Potoroo, a species found only in wet forests in far-eastern Victoria, was described as recently as 1981.

Perhaps the most ubiquitous of the kangaroos of the wet forests is the Swamp Wallaby. This species is predominantly a browser and eats a great variety of plants. Indeed, it has been known to eat some plants that are poisonous to stock without suffering any ill effects. While very common throughout eastern Australia, this species is unknown in Tasmania where the Tasmanian Pademelon takes its place.

As the tall forests give way to more open, grassy forest on poorer ground or drier areas, the diversity of kangaroos increases. Where there is dense ground cover, the Long-nosed Potoroo can be found. It eats almost no green matter but spends its time beneath dense bushes searching for the fungi that are the main component of its diet.

In more open areas one of the three species of *Bettongia* may be found. These beautiful little rat-kangaroos were once wide-spread outside of the tropics in Australia. But today, in part because of the introduction of the fox and because of habitat alteration, all of the *Bettongia* species are rare on the mainland. Only in Tasmania (where there are no foxes) can one be confident of encountering these exquisite animals. Curiously they build nests out of plant material that they carry curled in their tails.

In woodlands in coastal Queensland is found a larger species of bettong that is placed in its own genus. The Rufous Rat-kangaroo (*Aepyprymnus rufescens*) is not as rare as the other species for reasons we do not fully understand.

Some of the largest living kangaroos inhabit woodlands. These species include the Eastern and Western Grey Kangaroos and the Antilopine Wallaroo. The two grey kangaroo species occur together only in small areas of their range, principally in western New South Wales, while the Eastern Grey Kangaroo and Antilopine Wallaroo occur together only in a small part of northeastern Queensland.

All of the large kangaroos of the forests are grass-eaters and among the most sociable of kangaroo species. The two grey kangaroo species were reported in the past to congregate in mobs composed of many hundreds of individuals. A plethora of smaller wallabies, which are related to the grey kangaroos, inhabit Australia's wood-

MIGHTY GUM AND EASTERN GREY KANGAROO: A FAMILIAR SIGHT IN EASTERN AUSTRALIA.

lands. By and large these species, collectively called brush wallabies, tend to replace each other geographically or occupy slightly different habitats. Perhaps the most striking of the brush wallabies is the Pretty-face Wallaby (*Macropus parryi*) of eastern Queensland and northeastern New South Wales. The contrasting horizontal striping of the face and long whip-like tail makes this species easy to identify. Pretty-face Wallabies are very sociable and are often seen in large groups in woodland and stony areas. As with the larger kangaroos, the males are much larger than the females and have very powerful forearms with which they grapple in "wrestling bouts" to establish dominance.

The only species of kangaroo unique to New South Wales is a species of brush wallaby, the Parma Wallaby (*Macropus parma*). One of the smallest of the brush wallabies, this species inhabits wet sclerophyll forests and was once found from near Wollongong in the south to the Dorrigo area in the north. For many years the species was not seen in New South Wales and it was thought to be extinct. Then in 1965 it was found that some animals had been transported to Kawau Island, New Zealand during the previous century. The descendants of these animals still live on Kawau, but until they were recognised as being rare and thought extinct in their native habitat, they were actively persecuted as pests! The story of the rediscovery of the Parma Wallaby has a surprising end, however, because soon after its discovery on Kawau Island, some animals were found in their original habitat in New South Wales. The species is now known to be thinly distributed in small parts of its original range.

The prettiest of the scrub wallabies, the Toolache Wallaby (*Macropus greyi*) is now extinct. This species has the dubious distinction of being the largest of the kangaroos to become extinct in recent times. At the time of European contact, the Toolache Wallaby was abundant in a small area of southeastern South Australia. Because of its beautiful pelt and because it was very fast and provided a good hunt, the species was persecuted relentlessly until, by the early 1920s, it was restricted to a very tiny area. Concerned people of the time tried to remove some of the survivors on Konetta sheep run to a sanctuary on Kangaroo Island. But because they used dogs to chase the animals, only four dead and dying animals were obtained. Ironi-

BIG ENOUGH TO FORAGE FOR HIMSELF, THIS YOUNG WALLABY STILL SEEKS OUT ITS MOTHER.

SILENT UNDER A BUSH THIS SPECTACLED HARE WALLABY WILL NOT MOVE UNTIL NEARLY STEPPED UPON.

cally, it was probably this solitary gesture of concern by Europeans that caused the final demise of the species.

The dense dry scrubs of Australia, such as the *Acacia* thickets, are home to several curious little wallabies. The two most remarkable species are found only in Western Australia and, indeed, are only common on islands off the coast.

The Banded Hare-wallaby (*Lagostrophus fasciatus*) is today found only on Bernier and Dorre Islands in Shark Bay, Western Australia. There it builds complex runways under the cover of dense *Acacia* thickets. The life history of the Banded Hare-wallaby is little-known but the species is remarkable in that it is the last survivor of a once vast radiation of large kangaroos (called the sthenurines) that were very abundant in prehistoric times. Future studies of this little-known species should shed considerable light on the way the giant kangaroos of Australia's past lived.

The second of Western Australia's unique little scrub dwellers is the better-known Quokka (*Setonix brachyurus*). This species is familiar to many tourists because it is found most abundantly on Rottnest Island, off Fremantle, Western Australia. Here it lives in dense scrubs but it can be approached quite closely because it has little fear of man. It can even be fed by hand. The origins of the Quokka are shrouded in mystery but there is some evidence that it may be related to the pademelons (*Thylogale*) of eastern Australia. Its distinctive short tail, which is less than twice the length of the head, makes the Quokka an easy animal to identify.

THE KANGAROOS OF THE DESERTS

Despite the forbidding aspect of Australia's deserts, a surprising number of kangaroo species have successfully adapted to life in the area. The desert-dwelling kangaroos vary in their strategies of coping with the rigors of the desert. Some species tend to avoid the greatest stresses of the desert by taking advantage of microhabitats, for example, by living in caves or burrows where the air is cool and humid, and only coming out to feed at night. These species differ little physiologically from species living in the better watered areas of Australia. Others, however, have confronted the challenge of desert life full on. They have adapted their physiology to cope with the worst of conditions.

Perhaps the most striking of all desert kangaroos is the Burrowing Bettong (*Bettongia lesueur*). As its name suggests this rat-kangaroo excavates large and complex burrow systems and is the only kangaroo to do so. The burrows interconnect to form warrens which are inhabited by several animals. In the early part of the twentieth century, it was reported that rabbits and Burrowing Bettongs shared warrens, the rabbits inhabiting the upper chambers and the bettongs the deeper ones. The Burrowing Bettongs emerge in the cool of night to feed on succulent plants from which they derive both food and water. The Burrowing Bettongs are among the noisiest of kangaroos and can emit loud grunts, snarls and squeals. Indeed, many bushmen knew them by the name "squeaker". Sadly, the Burrowing Bettong is now extinct on the Australian mainland, probably because of the introduction of European animals. Today it survives only on some small islands off the Western Australian coast.

Other desert species include some rock-wallabies and euros. These species are found throughout much of Australia wherever rocky areas exist. They keep cool by day by resting in deep rock crevasses and caves. Because they are tied to their rocky homes one of their main problems is access to water. Rock-wallabies will drink from shallow pools after a brief shower. However, they must drink rapidly as the pools often dry up after an hour or two. Euros often arrange their territories in a cartwheel-shaped pattern centering on a waterhole so that the maximum number of individuals have access to water. Euros can survive where there is no water but only in low numbers and where food and deep caves are sufficient.

Some hare-wallabies (species of *Lagorchestes*) are desert-dwellers. They dig shallow burrows during the heat of summer, but shelter under bushes for much of the year. Three of the four species of hare-wallaby have suffered a sad decline since European settlement and two, the Eastern Hare-wallaby (*Lagorchestes leporides*) and the Central Hare-wallaby (*Lagorchestes asomatus*) are probably extinct. The hare-wallabies are remarkable leapers and John Gould, an early naturalist, reported that one leapt clear over his head. Indeed, leaps of up to 1.8 m have been reported, a great achievement for an animal that stands about 30 cm high! The extinction of the desert-dwelling hare-wallabies may well be linked to the destruction of the traditional Aboriginal culture. Desert Aborigines constantly burned small

THE FEMALE RED KANGAROO – CALLED A BLUE FLIER – IS HARD TO SPOT IN A SALT BUSH PLAIN.

patches of vegetation, both to hunt and to clear the country. The hare-wallabies apparently need the vegetation mosaic thus created to survive. They would use the unburned areas with old bushes for shelter, and more recently burned areas with younger bushes and freshly sprouted grass for feeding. Today huge fires periodically ravage vast areas of central Australia, creating uniform vegetation patterns. The Western Hare-wallaby (*Lagorchestes hirsutus*) survives today only where Aboriginal land management practices were carried out in the recent past. The National Parks and Wildlife Service is now encouraging Aborigines to burn the bush surrounding these areas as they did in the past, to ensure the survival of this species.

The Crescent Nailtail Wallaby (*Onychogalea lunata*) is yet another species that has adapted to desert life. It appears to have inhabited scrubs and was found in the ranges around Alice Springs as well as in the Goldfields and Wheatbelt regions of Western Australia. This pretty little wallaby is now extinct and we know almost nothing about its habits. Various early collectors report, however, that it would clamber up the insides of burned out trees when chased.

Two species of kangaroos represent the epitome of adaptation to desert life. These are the Red Kangaroo (*Macropus rufus*), the largest of kangaroo species, and the Desert Rat-kangaroo (*Caloprymnus campestris*) which is among the smallest of kangaroos. The Red Kangaroo is an inhabitant of the arid inland plains of Australia. Because it can find little shade and is highly active, the Red Kangaroo needs access to water. The provision of bores for stock throughout Australia has been a great boon to the Red Kangaroo and the species is now seen in greater numbers than ever before. It is now the most abundant of desert-dwelling kangaroos. The Red Kangaroo is the most intensely studied kangaroo species and we know much about its reproduction and physiology.

In contrast to the much studied and well-known Red Kangaroo, the Desert Rat-kangaroo is one of the most poorly-known of all kangaroo species. When it was first discovered by collectors working for John Gould in the 1840s, they did not mention it was rare or in any way extraordinary. However, it was then not heard of or seen for the following 90 years. Then, in 1931, the noted zoologist Hedley Finlayson from the South Australian Museum found it to be abundant in the north-eastern part of South Australia. However, after

BUILT FOR SPEED, A RED KANGAROO FLIES ACROSS THE DESERT PLAIN.

THE BLACK-FOOTED ROCK WALLABY, SAFE IN HIS ROCKY RAMPART.

1935 the species had again become rare and it has not been seen since. While it may well be extinct, occasional reports by graziers from the northeast of South Australia of "kangaroo rats" indicate that it may still survive in remote areas. After all, it was completely unknown for 90 years and then suddenly became abundant. This suggests it may be a "plague species" which survives in some small refuge when conditions are unfavourable, but which spreads rapidly when conditions are right. The Desert Rat-kangaroo inhabits gibber plains and sand dunes in the driest areas of South Australia. The only shelter that it was known to use was the shade of a sparse desert bush. The physiological adaptations that allowed this little animal to survive in some of Australia's harshest deserts remain totally unknown.

It can be seen from the above that the kangaroos are among the most diverse and successful of all Australian marsupials. While some have suffered range reductions and extinction at the hand of European Man and his introduced animals, others such as the Red Kangaroo have benefited from European-wrought changes. Indeed, some kangaroo species have extended their range to overseas. Feral populations of Red-necked Wallabies are now living in Scotland, Germany and New Zealand, and Rock-wallabies have established themselves in Hawaii. Perhaps in the distant future kangaroos will adapt themselves to many environments in their new homes, for given the adaptations they have evolved up to now, little seems to be beyond the bounds of possibility.

"Out West, where the stars are brightest,
Where the scorching north wind blows,
And the bones of the dead gleam whitest,
And the sun on a desert glows —"

FROM *THE GREAT GREY PLAIN*, HENRY LAWSON, 1893

A RED KANGAROO, EARS ALERT, IS ON THE MOVE FOR AN ACTIVE NIGHT.

Page 58–59. BARELY A STOCK OF SHADE EXISTS TO OFFER RELIEF FOR THESE RED KANGAROOS.

WESTERN GREY KANGAROOS AT A DESERT WATERHOLE.

WRESTLING ESTABLISHES DOMINANCE AMONG MALE RED KANGAROOS.

A 'MOB' OF EASTERN GREY KANGAROOS.

SAFE IN THE POUCH, A JOEY GREY KANGAROO SURVEYS THE WORLD.

PADEMELONS...HALF WRESTLING, HALF PLAYING.

HIDDEN BY DAY IN THE RAINFOREST THIS PADEMELON WILL EMERGE AT NIGHT TO FEED AT THE FOREST EDGE.

RABBIT-LIKE, A RED KANGAROO SPRINTS HEAD-ON.

OLD MAN RED KANGAROO... PATRIARCH OF THE ENDLESS INLAND PLAINS.

STARTLED AGILE WALLABIES LOOK UP FROM FEEDING.

A MALE WESTERN AUSTRALIAN WALLAROO DISPLAYS HIS MASSIVE FORELIMBS, AMONG THE MOST POWERFUL OF ALL KANGAROOS.

THE SWAMP WALLABY OF EASTERN AUSTRALIA EATS ALMOST ANYTHING.

A RED KANGAROO BOUNDS EFFORTLESSLY ACROSS A GIBBER PLAIN.

AN UPRIGHT KANGAROO IS DIFFICULT TO SPOT IN A DENSE FOREST.

A GREY KANGAROO ENJOYS THE EARLY MORNING SUN.

A TAMMAR WALLABY IN THE DENSE COASTAL SCRUB.

A PADEMELON IN THE GLOOMY RAINFOREST.

THE ELEGANT PRETTY-FACE WALLABY.

A BLACK-FOOTED ROCK WALLABY AT SIMPSON'S GAP IN THE NORTHERN TERRITORY.

THE MIGHTY MALE RED KANGAROO SHOWS OFF HIS BICEPS.

THE FEMALE RED KANGAROO IS FAR MORE DELICATELY BUILT THAN HER MUSCULAR MATE.

EVER WARY: THE KEY TO SURVIVAL.

A SMALL GROUP OF EASTERN GREY KANGAROOS.

AN AGILE WALLABY IN A RIVERSIDE HABITAT.

A JOEY GREY KANGAROO PLAYFULLY BOXES HIS MOTHER'S EARS.

EVERY MUSCLE OF THE RED KANGAROO IS TENSED FOR ANOTHER MIGHTY BOUND AWAY.

"Whole years go by when the glowing
Sky never clouds for rain —
Only the shrubs of the desert
Grow on The Great Grey Plain."

FROM *THE GREAT GREY PLAIN*, HENRY LAWSON, 1893

THE KANGAROO AND MANKIND

The Arrival of the Aborigines

WHO WERE the first Australians and when did they arrive on the then virgin continent? These questions have occupied scientists for more than 100 years and even today there are may competing theories regarding these matters. UIntil about 40 years ago many scientists believed that Aborigines had only been in Australia for a short time, certainly not more than 15,000 years. Today we know that Aborigines arrived in Australia at least 40,000 years ago, but some think that they have been here much longer; perhaps for as long as 120,000 years.

As to *who* the first Australians were, this question is at least as problematic as when they arrived. Many scientists believe that the modern Australian Aborigines are the descendents of later invaders who displaced the original inhabitants, or that they are the result of a mixing of several racial types which arrived in Australia at different times. Whatever the case, it is widely accepted that the original home of the first Australians was probably southeast Asia.

The sea journey that led to the first settlement of Australia was surely at least as epic an undertaking as Cook's voyage of discovery. For, 40,000 or more years ago, only the most rudimentary vessels existed. The first Australians probably covered the open sea between Australia and Asia (which must have been at least 150 km apart, even at times of the lowest sea level) in canoes or rafts. We can imagine the anxiety of those first Aboriginal adventurers, afloat on the sea, possibly for days, not knowing what, if anything, lay at the journey's end. The uniqueness of this voyage becomes apparent when we consider where people had *not* reached 40,000 years ago. The Americas, Madagascar, many islands of the Mediterranean, Micronesia and New Zealand, among others, were all uninhabited. Stories of the voyage must have been handed down from generation to generation, but sometime in the past they became lost or changed beyond recognition. To some extent they were replaced by tales of how things uniquely Australian came to be and how the Aborigines fitted into this new landscape.

Upon their arrival these first Australians were surely surprised at the unique Australian fauna that had evolved in isolation over the previous 40 million years. We can imagine the feeling of wonder mixed with fear that they must have felt when they confronted for the first time the gigantic and now extinct kangaroos and other animals that then populated Australia. Doubtless, though, they soon learned how to take advantage of such easily won protein, and thus began a period of ecological instability as the new predator, *Homo sapiens*, and the Australian fauna began to interact. Many species of gigantic marsupial became extinct between 40,000 and 20,000 years ago, and it seems likely that the coming of the Aborigines to Australia was an important factor in those events. Indeed, it would be surprising if this were not the case. Man is a highly efficient predator and we have seen the changes that have been wrought in Australia by the Europeans and in New Zealand by the Maoris who caused the extinction of the moas. The Australian fauna and the early Australians achieved a stable ecological balance during this period. By the time the Europeans arrived, this balance had long been struck. This is evidenced in part by the fact that no Australian mammal that we know of had become extinct in the 10,000 years before the coming of the Europeans.

In coming to terms with the new environment it seems probable that the Aborigines actually maintained the landscape so that important food species were advantaged. The technique used by the Aborigines has been dubbed "firestick farming" because fire was the most important tool in their management of the environment. By burning small patches of vegetation at the right times of year the Aborigines encouraged the growth of certain plants that were food for many kangaroos and other edible species. This burning pattern also ensured that large wildfires did not ravage the landscape, and the patchwork pattern that ensued provided animals with both unburned protective cover and good feed.

It is not really surprising that such a system evolved, for the Aborigines were dependent upon the Australian animals that firestick farming aided. The large kangaroos were particularly important, for their skins were used as cloaks and waterbags, sinews for binding, bones for barbs and speartips, and teeth for decoration. What's more, a kangaroo carcass could provide a feast for a group comprising several families.

Sadly, the Aboriginal way of life has long since disappeared over much of the continent. However, today we can learn much about

LAND CLEARING AND NEW WATERHOLES MAY HAVE INCREASED THE NUMBER OF GREY KANGAROOS.

the Aborigines and how they viewed the land and its wildlife from the many legends and tales that have been recorded. Some of the stories tell of the time before, when the boundaries between men and animals were blurred, and even of times before there were any kangaroos at all.

One often told Aboriginal legend recounts how the kangaroos first arrived in Australia. It is said that in the Dreamtime there were no kangaroos and the people had to eat yams, fruit and whatever small game they could catch. Then one day a huge storm blew up. The wind was so powerful that small animals were carried into the sky. A hunting party that was out when the storm arrived saw among the debris and leaves in the sky some large and strange animals. They had small front legs but very long back legs that seemed to reach to the ground. Suddenly the wind dropped and the huge animals fell to earth. Here they shook themselves and quickly bounded off. The amazed hunters were delighted, for these were the largest animals that they had ever seen. They went back to their families and after relating what they had seen, went off in pursuit of the strange game. However, it was a long time before the men learned how to catch these strange and fast animals. But when they finally did succeed, there was more than enough food for everyone.

Other Aboriginal legends tell of a time when the kangaroo went on all fours and of how he began to hop. Yet others tell of how an old paperbark tree stump turned into a kangaroo. Indeed, there are a great many Aboriginal stories that explain how the kangaroo came to be the way he is. A few even tell of how some of the various kinds of kangaroo became different.

The Aborigines of South Australia explained why the Red Kangaroo and Euro are indifferent to each other and live in separate habitats in the following story. Long ago there was a Red Kangaroo man, Wudli, and a Euro man, Munya, who were great friends. By day they would search for food and in the evening come together to discuss the day's events. One day Wudli found a large patch of yams. However, being a mean and scheming fellow, he did not tell his friend of his good fortune. As time went by Wudli became sleek and fat on the yams, but because Munya could find little food he was reduced to skin and bones. Munya became suspicious that Wudli was hiding food from him, and the next morning followed him out

GREY KANGAROOS ON FARMLAND.

of camp. When he found Wudli eating the yams he became very angry and abused his friend for not sharing the food. Wudli then attacked Munya, but he scratched and bit Wudli so badly that Wudli tried to run away. However, every time he tried to do so, Munya dragged him back by the legs. As a result, his legs stretched, and even today the legs of the Red Kangaroo are longer than those of the Euro. The two fought until they were exhausted and then Wudli, making good his escape, hopped into the middle of a broad plain where he laid down to recover. Munya, however, could find no rest, for he was lying on a small stone. Munya blew on the stone and it grew and grew until it formed the Flinders Ranges of South Australia. Munya thought that the new mountain range was a good place to live, and ever since Euros have lived in hilly areas. Wudli saw the advancing ranges and thought that they might cover his home, so he pushed them back with one sweep of this tail to where they lie today. From that day to this, the Red Kangaroo and the Euro have had nothing to do with each other, one living in the mountain ranges and the other on the plains.

Among the most delightful of Aboriginal legends are those that teach children how to treat the land and its animals properly. Daisy Bates recorded one such tale. She was told that in the Dreamtime a group of people who lived in the southwest of the country shared the land with a great kangaroo spirit that made sure everyone obeyed the law. The people were forbidden to kill little kangaroos. Instead they were instructed to treat them as if they were their own children. Above all, the people were not to mock or imitate kangaroos. One day when the men were hunting, a group of little boys found a nest of hopping mice. They killed the baby mice and, pretending that they were kangaroo hunters and that the baby mice were baby kangaroos, they butchered them as the men would butcher a large kangaroo. When the mice parents returned home they were distraught to find their babies gone. When they told the kangaroo spirit of the boys' naughtiness, the spirit was so angry that he asked another spirit to form a great lake where the tribe camped, and all the people were drowned. It can be seen by this terrible retribution how important tribal laws relating to large game animals such as kangaroos were to the Aborigines.

THE QUOKKA BENEFITS FROM MAN'S DEBRIS ON ROTTNEST ISLAND.

It was respect for their environment perpetuated in tales such as these, along with food taboos, that helped the Aborigines to live in ecological harmony with their environment for thousands of years. But explorers with a very different cultural background were to reach the shores of Australia. Their arrival as permanent settlers in 1788 heralded the beginning of a new period of instability and change over the face of Australia that was to be at least as traumatic as the period of ecological instability between 40,000 and 20,000 years ago.

The Coming of the Europeans

After the Aborigines and the New Guineans, the next human to see a kangaroo was probably an itinerant South East Asian. These people had been visiting the northern coast of Australia to collect trepang (a kind of echinoderm) for hundreds of years before Cook visited Australia's east coast. Unfortunately, because they have left no accounts of their voyages, we will never know exactly what wildlife these early visitors saw in the new land.

One of the first Europeans to see a kangaroo was probably Diego d Prado y Tovar, a Portuguese mariner who accompanied the explorer Torres after whom the Torres Strait is named. In 1606, Diego and Torres were sailing along the southern coast of New Guinea when a strange animal (possibly a Dusky Pademelon, *Thylogale brunii*) was brought aboard ship. Inspired by scientific curiosity, Diego commented on the unusual nature of the animal's tail and testicles, but then, overcome by baser instincts, he ate the object of his studies.

This early encounter between European and kangaroo seems to have set the trend for most subsequent interactions. The early explorers' accounts are liberally sprinkled with tales of the then new and unusual kangaroos as well as comments about their culinary value. Thus when Joseph Banks saw his first kangaroo in 1770 he wrote ". . . It is different from any . . . animal I have heard or read of except the Jerbua of Egypt . . . It may however be easily known from all other animals by the singular property of running or rather hopping upon only its hinder legs carrying its fore bent close to its breast." He later noted that he ". . . Dined today upon the animal, who eat but ill, he was I suppose too old. His fault, however was an

GREY KANGAROOS: TRYING TO ESTABLISH A NEW ECOLOGICAL BALANCE WITH MANKIND.

uncommon one, the total want of flavour, for he certainly was the most insipid meat I eat . . .".

Many early accounts are remarkable for the difficulty that European observers had in describing kangaroos. The Dutch navigator Volckertzoon described the Quokka (*Setonix brachyurus*) of Rottnest Island as ". . . a wild cat, resembling a Civet cat, but with browner hair . . .". Vlamingh, the Dutchman who gave Rottnest its name, called the island after the Quokkas which he evidently thought were rats. The famous English pirate and gentleman William Dampier called the Banded Hare-wallaby (*Lagostrophus fasciatus*) ". . . a sort of Raccoon . . ." which was ". . . very good meat . . .". That these accounts seem to neglect the most obvious features of kangaroos is probably due to the difficulty that anyone would have when asked to describe such an alien animal. In their descriptions of them as cats, rats or raccoons, these early explorers neglected the features of these animals that to later observers indicated their unique nature.

After 1770, these quaint, albeit inaccurate accounts of kangaroos began to give way to more exhaustive and accurate descriptions. Indeed, 1770 is a momentous year in our association with kangaroos because it was in that year that Captain Cook first recorded the name "kangaroo" for an animal that he caught near Cooktown. The original meaning of the word kangaroo is now shrouded in mystery. It may be that the Cooktown Aborigines completely misunderstood Cook's question about the name of the animal he had caught. It is even possible that they in fact were giving Cook the name of the surrounding country. Whatever the case, "kangaroo" was one of the first (if not the first) Aboriginal words to become incorporated into the English language, and today it is certainly the most widespread of all Aboriginal words.

It is perhaps just as well that Cook was forced to stop on the north Queensland coast to repair the damaged *Endeavour*. Otherwise he might have left Australia without having seen a kangaroo. If this had happened, this book might have been about "Patagarangs", which is the term used by the Aborigines of the Port Jackson area for the Eastern Grey Kangaroo (*Macropus giganteus*).

Before about 1850, European contact with kangaroos probably had a minimal effect on kangaroo numbers. However, in the following hundred years the spread of agriculture and our ancestors' deter-

A RED-NECKED WALLABY RAISES THE FLAG.

mination to turn Australia into a "little England", had a drastic effect on the native mammalian fauna. Areas worst affected were the semi-arid regions, particularly in western New South Wales and the wheatbelt of Western Australia. By the early 1890s, such areas were badly overstocked with sheep; western New South Wales alone harboured over 15 million. Because of drought, rabbits and permanent damage done to the soil and vegetation by overgrazing, this area has never subsequently been able to carry half that number of sheep.

Such massive environmental degradation had tragic effects on many of the kangaroos of these areas. Western New South Wales was once home to Burrowing Bettongs (*Bettongia lesueur*), Brush-tailed Bettongs (*Bettongia penicillata*), Rufous Bettongs (*Aepyprymnus rufescens*), Eastern Hare Wallabies (*Lagorchestes leporides*) and Bridled Nailtail Wallabies (*Onychogalea fraenata*). All of these are now gone from this area, most having vanished before the turn of the century. These species did not decline because of excessive shooting or hunting; rather they were the victims of the habitat changes directly or indirectly caused by Europeans. Lack of understanding and greed, not bloodthirstiness, were the main factors responsible for the decline.

Not every kangaroo species was adversely affected by these changes. The modification of much of Australia's semi-arid land into suitable grazing country allowed the Red Kangaroo to go from an uncommon and rarely seen animal to one of the country's most abundant large mammals. In some areas it reaches plague proportions, and western New South Wales is one of the areas where this species is now most abundant. Ironically, more than 100 years ago, the English naturalist John Gould predicted the imminent demise of the Red Kangaroo. However, it is the small and unobtrusive species which he presumed to be safe that are now extinct or gone from most of their range.

While the European settlement of western New South Wales provides the starkest example of how we have affected the fortunes of kangaroos, other areas have been affected in different ways. Although it is clear that the species of kangaroo inhabiting higher rainfall areas have fared much better than desert-dwelling forms, the fates of the two kangaroo species from forested eastern Australia that have been most adversely affected by European activity are worth considering. Their decline is indicative of other ways in which

AN UNWELCOME VISITOR TO AUSTRALIAN FARMLANDS.

GREY KANGAROOS MAKE EASY PREY FOR THE HUNTER.

we have affected the Australian fauna.

The Toolache Wallaby (*Macropus greyi*) is the largest macropodid to have become extinct since European settlement. Factors that made it so vulnerable were its restricted distribution, its beautiful pelt and its attractiveness as the quarry in a kangaroo hunt. The small portion of southeastern South Australia that was home to this species was an attractive area for sheep grazing. Because of this, it was not long before Europeans moved in *en masse*. Frederick Wood Jones recalls seeing hundreds of its beautiful skins for sale in Adelaide and also recounts how its fleetness of foot made it much better sport to chase than the other kangaroo species. Against this unrelenting persecution and habitat modification, the Toolache never really stood a chance. It had no refuge such as offshore islands or remote areas where it could survive. Shot and hunted until the end, the last Toolache died in 1939. Fortunately, this seems to be the only case where a species of kangaroo has been hunted into extinction by Europeans.

In curious contrast is the case of the Tasmanian Bettong (*Bettongia gaimardi*). This species was widespread in southeastern Australian and Tasmanian sclerophyll forests at the time of European settlement. Although a few were probably eaten in the early days of settlement by struggling pioneers, the species was never persecuted. Nonetheless it quickly became rare and was extinct on mainland Australia by 1900. Luckily, the species still survives in moderate numbers in Tasmania. As large areas of apparently suitable habitat for the species still exist on the mainland, habitat alteration does not appear to have been a major factor in its decline. There is some evidence, however, that the introduction of a single European species, the Red Fox (*Vulpes vulpes*) may have been responsible for its demise. We know that the Fox has had a drastic effect on the numbers of related bettong species elsewhere in Australia. The survival of the Tasmanian Bettong only in Tasmania may well be due to the fact that the Fox was never introduced there.

The decline and extinction of Australian kangaroos seems to be due to a number of factors. Some species were clearly more vulnerable than others to various forms of environmental disturbance. On the other hand, although many European activities have adversely affected some species, others seem to have benefited from them.

Many of us like to feel that the fate of other animals depends on us, but too many fail to recognise that the opposite is also true: we depend on other animals. For example, Aborigines and pioneers were, from time to time dependent on kangaroo meat for food, and even today the livelihood of some people in the outback depends on kangaroo products. Conversely, an excess of kangaroos can threaten the livelihood of the grazier. In the future, we may become even more dependent on the kangaroo. If we find, as some already suggest, that the hard-footed introduced mammals that we now eat are too destructive to central Australia's delicate ecosystems, then we may well be forced to turn to an alternate source for protein. Kangaroos have had over 15 million years to evolve an ideal and efficient lifestyle for this continent. What better animals could we find to form the basis of an efficient and ecologically sound meat industry? If we do not explore this avenue central Australia could one day be turned into a vast desert by our herds of sheep and cows.

THE SPECIES OF AUSTRALIA AND NEW GUINEA

THE SPECIES ACCOUNTS

In the sections that follow we have attempted to use standard procedures in the presentation of data. The kangaroo measurements given for each species include all the available statistics, and in some cases are incomplete simply because the data does not exist. Nose-vent is the distance from the tip of the nose to the cloacal vent when the animal is stretched out belly-up with its head tipped back. Tail-vent is the distance from the tip of the tail (flesh, not hair) to the cloacal vent. Hindfoot is the length of the hindfoot measured along the sole from the posterior edge of the heel to the base of the claw of the longest toe (which is the fourth toe in kangaroos). Ear is the length of the ear measured as the distance from the base of the notch to the tip of the pinna.

Obtaining these measurements is not always easy. Some of those recorded here come from the original descriptions of the species, some from museum labels and some from the summaries given in the species accounts in Strahan (1983). They are very rarely representative for the whole species but serve to give some idea of the size of the animal.

The biological information has similarly been compiled from a wide variety of sources. Notable among these are the summary works of Gould (1863), Jones (1924), Frith and Calaby (1969), Ride (1970), Groves and Ride (1982) and Strahan (1983) and Ziegler (1983). Additional sources include a work in preparation by Archer on the mammals of eastern Australia to be published by the Queensland Museum. (These standard references are listed following the species accounts.)

The basis for determination of the conservation status of the Australian species in large part follows Ride and Wilson (1982) with most departures being based on the accounts in Strahan (1983), other more recent studies or the work in preparation by Archer. The basis for similar determinations for the New Guinean mammals is George (1979). Departures from this are otherwise based on work in preparation by Flannery.

The distribution maps are similarly a compilation from various source materials. The principal sources for the Australian species were the accounts in Strahan (1983). These were modified by reference to more recent studies as well as to detailed distribution notes compiled and kindly made available by Dr A. Robinson. The distribution maps for New Guinean mammals were compiled using original data as well as that available in the literature (e.g., Groves 1982).

The literature references given after each account are far from exhaustive. They are provided as an aid to any reader who wishes to delve more deeply into the subject. We have also avoided repetitive listing of certain standard references preferring to list them here in a geographically relevant context.

A Guide To The Following Maps
The habitats of the species are represented in the following guide by maps. The dark grey zone shows the present distributions; the pink zone represents the possible former distribution.

SPECIES OF AUSTRALIA

MUSKY RAT-KANGAROO

Hypsiprymnodon moschatus

STATUS: VULNERABLE

SIZE

Nose-vent: *M* 23.0cm (15.3–27.3); *F* 23.3cm (21.2–25.2)
Tail-vent: *M* 14.5cm (13.2–15.9); *F* 14.0cm (12.3–15.3)
Hindfoot (s.u.): *M* 5.5cm
Ear (n.): *M* 2.9cm
Adult weight: *M* 0.5kg (0.3–0.7); *F* 0.5kg (0.5–0.6)

This rarely seen rainforest species is the most primitive living kangaroo. It retains a first toe on its hind foot, a feature otherwise lost during the evolutionary history of the other kangaroos and, unlike other kangaroos, it gallops rather than hops.

It has a very distinctive toothrow suggesting the possibility that its diet of fruits, seeds and small animals differs very little from a recently discovered species of the genus that is about 15 million years old.

These rat-kangaroos are also the only species of kangaroo to regularly give birth to twins. Breeding occurs between the months of February and July. After birth, the young stay in the pouch for about 21 weeks and do not reach sexual maturity until about one year old.

They normally live in globular nests built of fallen leaves. Here they spend the nights and the middle parts of the day. After the young leave the pouch, they spend considerable time in the female's nest.

The rainforest in which they occur covers an area of only about 320 by 65km. For this reason alone, they are highly vulnerable to any alterations that might occur to their restricted habitat.

REFERENCES

Carlsson, A., 1915. Zur morphologie des *Hypsiprymnodon moschatus*.
Kungl. Svenska Vetenskapsakademiens Hanglingar 52(6):1–48.

Johnson, P.M. and Haffenden, A.T., 1983. Husbandry of the
Musky Rat-kangaroo in captivity. *J. Aust. Anim. Tech. Assoc.* 8:1–8.

Johnson, P.M. and Strahan, R., 1982. A further description of the Musky Rat-kangaroo,
Hypsiprymnodon moschatus Ramsay, 1876 (Marsupialia, Potoroidae), with notes on its biology. *Aust. Zool.* 21:27–46.

118

BROAD-FACED POTOROO

Potorous platyops

STATUS: EXTINCT

SIZE

Nose-vent: *F* 30.5cm
Tail-vent: *F* 17.8cm
Hindfoot (s.u.): *F* 5.4cm
Ear (n.): *F* 2.2cm

This tiny species is the second most poorly-known of all Australian kangaroos (the least-known being the Central Hare-wallaby). It was collected from only a few localities in southwestern Western Australia, between 1839 and sometime prior to 1875. After that date, it was never seen alive again. Although there is a report that one was on display in the London Zoo in 1908, this has now generally been assumed to have been a juvenile Quokka (*Setonix brachyurus*).

Bones found on the surface of some of the Nullarbor caves, in caves on Kangaroo Island and caves in southern mainland South Australia indicate that not long before Europeans arrived, this potoroo was much more widely spread. What caused its decline is a complete mystery but it is at least some comfort to realize that responsibility for this recent decline appears not to be ours.

Virtually nothing is known about its biology except that it does not appear to have occupied forests. John Gilbert, the gatherer of one of the specimens from the interior of Western Australia, commented that it was killed in a "thicket" around a "salt lagoon".

REFERENCES

Butler, W.H. and Merrilees, D., 1971. Remains of *Potorous platyops* (Marsupialia, Macropodidae) and other mammals from Bremer Bay, Western Australia. *J. Proc. R. Soc. West. Aust.* 54:53–58.

Calaby, J.H., 1971. The current status of Australian Macropodidae. *Aust. Zool.* 16:17–29.

LONG-FOOTED POTOROO

Potorous longipes

STATUS: ENDANGERED

SIZE

Nose-vent: *M* 39.5cm (37.9–41.0); *F* 41.5cm
Tail-vent: *M* 31.9cm (31.5–32.0); *F* 32.0cm
Hindfoot (s.u.): *M* 10.7cm (10.3–11.4); *F* 10.7cm
Ear (n.): *M* 4.7cm (4.6–4.7); *F* 4.5cm (4.4–4.5)
Adult weight: *M* 2.1kg; *F* 1.7kg (1.6–1.8)

It is rare for new species of mammals to be discovered in Australia almost two centuries after European settlement and even rarer to discover a new one in the well-settled state of Victoria. In fact, until discovery of this large Victorian potoroo, no new mammals had been found in that State since 1888.

It was first caught near Bonang in a dog-trap. Barely a year later, a second specimen was found dead on the highway at Bellbird. Then in 1978, two were live-trapped at Bellbird. To date, a total of nine individuals from only three localities have been obtained, so it is clearly not a very common animal. Attempts are being made now by the Fisheries and Wildlife Division of Victoria to start a breeding colony in captivity.

In the "old" days, zoologists recognized new species by noting differences only in the morphology of the skulls or teeth or in the colour of the skin. Recognition of this new potoroo, like many other Australian mammals that have been recently recognized, was also based partly on the study of this potoroo's enzymes. Biochemical studies of this sort are proving to be among the best indicators of species distinctions.

REFERENCES
Seebeck, J.H. and Johnson, P.G., 1980. *Potorous longipes* (Marsupialia:Macropodidae);
a new species from eastern Victoria. *Aust. J. Zool.* 28:119–34.

LONG-NOSED POTOROO

Potorous tridactylus

STATUS: SECURE

SIZE

Nose-vent: *M* 41.0cm; *F* 34.0cm
Tail-vent: *M* 19.4cm (17.5–23.0); *F* 18.4cm (16.1–20.1)
Hindfoot (s.u.): *M* 8.2cm (7.7–8.5); *F* 7.6cm (7.1–7.9)
Ear (n.): *M* 4.0cm (3.5–4.3); *F* 4.0cm (4.0–4.1)
Adult weight: *M* 1.1kg (0.7–2.1); *F* 1.0kg (0.7–1.8)

At the time of European settlement, these rat-kangaroos occurred in southwestern Western Australia and South Australia as well as in the other states where they still survive. The only specimen reported from South Australia was noted in 1888 and the last record from Western Australia was 1840. Today they are rare in Queensland, of uncertain status in Victoria and New South Wales, but common in Tasmania. The reasons for their decline are not understood but it seems safe to say that in the long run, the responsibility was probably ours.

They prefer well-watered habitats including rainforests and wet sclerophyl forests. Evidently they also need relatively thick ground cover. Here they spend the day in shallow depressions dug into the ground.

They eat mostly fungi but also indulge in insects, sedges, some grasses and even snails. In captivity they eat a much wider range of fruits, vegetables and meat, demonstrating a decidedly omnivorous approach to things edible.

These potoroos breed twice a year throughout the year but a peak in births occurs in late winter. After a gestation period of 38 days, the 0.4gm new-born young takes 10 minutes to crawl from the mother's cloaca to her pouch. After about 150 days, the young are weaned. One captive lived for nine years and nine months.

REFERENCES

Guiler, E.R., 1971. Food of the potoroo (Marsupialia, Macropodidae). *J. Mammal.* 52:232–34.

Heinsohn, G.E., 1968. Habitat requirements and reproductive potential of the macropod marsupial *Potorous tridactylus* in Tasmania. *Mammalia* 32:30–43.

Johnston, P.G. and Sharman, G.B., 1977. Studies on populations of *Potorous* Desmarest (Marsupialia) II. Electrophoretic, chromosomal and breeding studies. *Aust. J. Zool.* 25:733–47.

Seebeck, J.H., 1981. *Potorous tridactylus* (Kerr) (Marsupialia:Macropodidae): its distribution, status and habitat preferences in Victoria. *Aust. Wildl. Res.* 8:285–306.

Ullmann, S.L. and Brown, R., 1983. Further observations on the Potoroo (*Potorous tridactylus*) in captivity. *Lab. Anim.* 17:133–37.

BURROWING BETTONG

Bettongia lesueur

STATUS: VULNERABLE

SIZE

Nose-vent: *M* and *F* 34.4cm (31.5–37.0)
Tail-vent: *M* and *F* 29.3cm (28.0–30.5)
Hindfoot (s.u.): *M* and *F* 10.1cm (9.6–10.4)
Ear (n.): *M* and *F* 3.5cm (3.1–3.9)
(Central Australian individuals)

This very delicate species has had a hard time since the arrival of Europeans. Its populations once spread across the continent from the islands off Western Australia to the edge of the Great Divide in New South Wales. Then, very soon after we introduced a host of noxious foreign mammals such as mice, rabbits, foxes, cats, cattle and so forth, the rot set in. By 1863 this delicate creature had vanished from Victoria and soon after from New South Wales (perhaps as early as 1892), South Australia (only a few left by the 1920s), the Northern Territory (gone by the 1930s) and finally from the mainland of Western Australia. Today it survives only on Barrow, Bernier, Boodie and Dorre Islands off the coast of northwestern Australia. On Boodie Island its survival is in severe jeopardy. It may be secure, however, on Bernier and Dorre Islands.

Of all kangaroos, this species is the only one that regularly digs and inhabits burrows. Some burrow systems, or warrens, have as many as 120 entrances and commonly each warren has at least half as many resident individuals as it has entrances.

Like other bettongs, this species commonly eats fungi, bulbs, roots and seeds, most of which it appears to detect with its keen sense of smell.

REFERENCES

Finlayson, H.H., 1958. On central Australian mammals (with notice of related species from adjacent tracts). Part III – The Potoroinae. *Rec. S. Aust. Mus.* 13:235–302.

Ride, W.D.L. and Tyndale-Biscoe, C.H., 1962. Mammals. *Fauna Bull. W. Aust. Fish. Dep. No.* 2:54–97.

Stodart, E., 1966. Observations on the behaviour of the marsupial *Bettongia lesueuri* (Quoy & Gaimard) in an enclosure. *C.S.I.R.O. Wildl. Res.* 11:91–99.

Tyndale-Biscoe, C.H., 1968. Reproduction and post-natal development in the marsupial *Bettongia lesueur* (Quoy & Gaimard). *Aust. J. Zool.* 16:577–602.

BRUSH-TAILED BETTONG

Bettongia penicillata

STATUS: ENDANGERED

SIZE

Nose-vent: *M* and *F* 33.0cm (30.0–38.0)
Tail-vent: *M* and *F* 31.0cm (29.0–36.0)
Hindfoot (s.u.): *F* 7.8cm
Ear (n.): *F* 2.8cm
Adult weight: *M* and *F* 1.3kg (1.1–1.6)

These small open forest and woodland rat-kangaroos appear to be masters at surviving bushfires. Much of their once widespread range was regularly and naturally subjected to bushfires. They appear to survive by racing madly ahead of the flames to patches of unburnt vegetation or by dashing back through the fire's edge to already burnt bush behind the fire's front.

Their diet is also unusual consisting of nothing green. Instead, they appear to use the fruiting bodies of underground fungi, bulbs, seeds, insects and even resin, possibly from *Hakea* shrubs.

Both their diet of fire-resistant foods and capacity to survive bushfires ironically appear to have made them bushfire-dependent. As a result, it has been suggested that long periods without bushfires would have a severe effect on their survival.

Like other rat-kangaroos, they build nests on the ground. Breeding occurs throughout the year. After birth, the single young stays in the pouch for about 90 days. It reaches sexual maturity by the time it is about 180 days.

This species was once very widespread but the depredations of foxes, competition with rabbits and possibly the interference of the normal fire-regime by man has radically restricted the species to a few tiny areas in southwestern Western Australia.

REFERENCES

Christensen, P., 1980. The biology of *Bettongia penicillata* Gray, 1837, and *Macropus eugenii* (Desmarest, 1817) in relation to fire. *Forests Dept. of West. Aust. Bull.* 91.

Christensen, P. and Leftwich, T., 1980. Observations on the nest-building habits of the Brush-tailed Rat-kangaroo or Woylie (*Bettongia penicillata*). *J. Proc. Roy. Soc. West. Aust.* 63:33–38.

Finlayson, H.H., 1958. On central Australian mammals (with notice of related species from adjacent tracts). Part III – The Potoroinae. *Rec. S. Aust. Mus.* 13:235–302.

King, D.R., Oliver, A.J. and Mead, R.J., 1981. *Bettongia* and fluoracetate: a role for 1080 in fauna management. *Aust. Wildl. Res.* 8:529–36.

Viola, S., 1977. Observations of the Brush-tailed Bettong at the New York Zoological Park. *Intern. Zoo Ybk.* 17:156–57.

TASMANIAN BETTONG

Bettongia gaimardi

STATUS: SECURE

SIZE

Nose-vent: *M* and *F* 32.3cm (31.5–33.2)
Tail-vent: *M* and *F* 32.6cm (28.8–34.5)
Hindfoot (s.u.): *M* 11.1cm (11.0–12.0); *F* 10.5cm
Ear (n.): *M* 3.5cm (2.9–4.0); *F* 3.0cm
Adult weight: *M* and *F* 1.7kg (1.2–2.3)

This beleaguered species lost its hold on the mainland at least 60 years ago. It was last collected in Queensland in about 1869 and in New South Wales in 1840. The Victorian and South Australian populations also followed suit. Today it only survives in Tasmania perhaps because of the relative rarity there of foxes and rabbits.

It prefers grassy plains and dry sclerophyll forests where it feeds on bulbous roots, grasses and tender shoots. Like other rat-kangaroos, it probably also eats small animals. Near human habitation, it has even been found eating kitchen scraps.

Shallow depressions are dug under the shelter of bushes or clumps of grass. In these they construct football-sized nests made of grass or strips of bark. Nest materials are transported from collection sites sometimes 0.4km away. They carry the nest materials in prehensile tails which they coil around the bundles of grass.

In captivity, young have been born in all months of the year except January and September. The gestation period is 21.1 days. At birth, the young weigh 0.3gm. The average period of time spent in the pouch is 109 days. One captive individual lived for eight years.

REFERENCES

Finlayson, H.H., 1959. On *Bettongia cuniculus* Ogilby, 1838. *Trans. R. Soc. S. Aust.* 82:283–89.

Kershaw, R.C., 1971. Notes on Tasmanian rat-kangaroos. *Vict. Nat.* 88:4–10.

Wakefield, N.A., 1976. Some taxonomic revision in the Australian marsupial genus *Bettongia* (Macropodidae), with description of a new species. *Vict. Nat.* 84:8–22.

LITTLE IS KNOWN OF THE NORTHERN BETTONG . . . OTHER THAN ITS RAINFOREST HABITAT.

NORTHERN BETTONG

Bettongia tropica

STATUS: VULNERABLE

SIZE

Nose-vent: *M* 33.7cm; *F* 30.6cm
Tail-vent: *M* 32.0cm; *F* 33.5cm
Hindfoot (s.u.): *M* 12.4cm; *F* 12.3cm
Ear (n.): *M* 3.8cm; *F* 4.0cm

Little is known about this species and even its specific distinction is disputed. It was first collected in 1884 by the noted zoologist and explorer Carl Lumholtz from the Dawson Valley in Queensland. Subsequent specimens were collected by P.J. Darlington in 1932 and by H.C. Raven in 1922 from rugged country in northeastern Queensland.

However, it was not until 1967 that it was named as a distinct species when N.A. Wakefield reviewed the whole genus. He noted features in the dentition, skull and pelage of these specimens that distinguished them from all others.

Now its status has been questioned again. A study of the chromosomes of a recently caught individual reveal that it is, in this regard, very similar to the Brush-tailed Bettong.

Nevertheless, the features of the teeth that Wakefield noted still suggest that it is not simply an isolated population of the Brush-tailed Bettong. For the moment, anyway, we consider it should be treated as a distinct species.

REFERENCES

Sharman, G.B., Murtagh, C.E., Johnson, P.M. and Weaver, C.M., 1980. The chromosomes of a rat-kangaroo attributable to *Bettongia tropica* (Marsupialia:Macropodidae). *Aust. J. Zool.* 28:59–63.

Wakefield, N.A. 1967. Some taxonomic revision in the Australian marsupial genus *Bettongia* (Macropodidae), with description of a new species. *Vict. Nat.* 84:8–22.

RUFOUS RAT-KANGAROO

Aepyprymnus rufescens

STATUS: SECURE

SIZE

Nose-vent: *M* 37.3cm (36.5–38.0); *F* 38.5cm (36.4–40.5)
Tail-vent: *M* 38.0cm (36.5–39.5); *F* 37.3cm (37.0–37.5)
Hindfoot (s.u.): *M* 13.6cm (13.4–13.8); *F* 13.6cm (13.2–14.0)
Ear (n.): *M* 5.5cm (5.3–5.7); *F* 5.1cm (4.6–5.5)
Adult weight: *M* 2.1kg (1.6–2.3); *F* 1.4–3.6kg

These spritely and often feisty potoroids are among the most engaging of the smaller kangaroos. They occur by preference in the open forests, woodlands and grasslands of eastern Australia. Here they feed on grasses, leaves and roots but are not at all adverse to eating insects and even bird eggs.

While once common in all of the eastern states except Tasmania, habitat destruction, the trademark of European man, has now reduced their range to northeastern New South Wales and eastern Queensland.

Adults live in dome-shaped grass nests built in depressions in the ground. After a gestation period of about 23 days, a single young is born which remains in the pouch for about 114 days. Young become sexually mature when they are about one year old and individuals may live for eight years.

Males are very aggressive towards each other and, although many individuals may be seen feeding together, for most of the rest of the time they are solitary. Between one and seven individuals per hectare have been seen in occupied areas depending on local conditions.

One of the most striking attributes of these kangaroos is their threat-call. When molested or otherwise aggravated, they produce a loud deep-throated droning noise that sounds remarkably like a chainsaw.

Natural predators include dingoes, quolls and owls but by far their most serious predator is now man.

REFERENCES

Finlayson, H.H., 1958. On central Australian mammals (with notice of related species from adjacent tracts).
Part III – The Potoroinae. *Rec. S. Aust. Mus.* 13:235–302.

Johnson, P.M., 1978. Reproduction in the Rufous Rat-kangaroo (*Aepyprymnus rufescens* (Gray))
in captivity with age estimation of pouch young. *Queensl. J. Agric. Anim. Sci.* 35:69–72.

Johnson, P.M., 1980. Observations of the behaviour of the Rufous Rat-kangaroo,
Aepyprymnus rufescens (Gray), in captivity. *Aust. Wildl. Res.* 7:347–57.

Moors, P.J., 1978. The urogenital system and notes on the reproductive biology of the female
Rufous Rat-kangaroo *Aepyprymnus rufescens* (Gray) (Macropodidae). *Aust. J. Zool.* 23:355–61.

DESERT RAT-KANGAROO

Caloprymnus campestris

STATUS: EXTINCT

SIZE

Nose-vent: *M* 38.1cm (33.2–44.0); *F* 26.7cm (25.4–27.7)
Tail-vent: *M* 37.0cm (36.0–38.0); *F* 33.5cm (31.0–37.7)
Hindfoot (su): *M* 12.0cm (11.9–12.1); *F* 10.9cm (10.4–11.5)
Ear (n): *M* 3.6cm (3.1–4.1); *F* 4.2cm (4.1–4.2)
Adult weight: *M* 0.8kg (0.6–0.9); *F* 1.0kg (0.7–1.1)

In 1843, John Gould saw no reason to worry about this tiny desert kangaroo. And yet, after his description, it was not seen again for almost a century. The rediscovery in South Australia in 1931 was announced by Hedley Finlayson in 1932 who described the chase (of the "oolacunta" as it was called by the local Aborigines): "Following the yell, Tommy came heading back down the line towards the sand-hill, but it was only after much straining of eyes that the oolacunta could be distinguished – a mere speck, thirty or forty yards ahead. At that distance it seemed scarcely to touch the ground; it almost floated ahead in an eerie, effortless way that made the thundering horse behind seem, by comparison, like a coal hulk wallowing in a heavy sea".

Unfortunately, soon after its rediscovery, this species floated out of sight again and has not been seen since.

The Aborigines used to locate this rat-kangaroo by recognizing its distinctive tracks on the sand-hills that were its home. Evidently when moving fast, unlike other kangaroos, its right foot struck the ground 7cm in front of the left and the left foot, unlike the right, always struck the ground obliquely.

Regrettably, apparent extinction overtook this delicate animal before its biological secrets of desert survival could be discovered.

REFERENCES

Finlayson, H.H., 1932. *Caloprymnus campestris*. Its recurrence and characters. *Trans. R. Soc. S. Aust.* 56:148–67.
Finlayson, H.H., 1935. "The red centre". Angus and Robertson:Sydney.
Finlayson, H.H., 1936. On mammals from the Lake Eyre Basin. Part III.
The diprotodont marsupials and Ornithodelphia. *Trans. Roy. Soc. S. Aust.* 60:157–61.
Finlayson, H.H., 1961. On central Australian mammals Part IV – The distribution and status of central Australian species. *Rec. S. Aust. Mus.* 14:141–91.

BANDED HARE-WALLABY

Lagostrophus fasciatus

STATUS: VULNERABLE

SIZE

Nose-vent: *M* and *F* 43.0cm (40.0–45.0)
Tail-vent: *M* and *F* 37.0cm (35.0–40.0)
Hindfoot (s.u.): *M* 10.0cm; *F* 9.5cm
Adult weight: *M* and *F* 1.3–3.0kg

This hare-wallaby has had a familiar history since its contact with Europeans. It was evidently abundant in areas of the mainland as late as the early 1900s but the last known mainland specimen was taken in 1906. Since then it has only been certainly known to occur on three off-shore islands: Dirk Hartog, Bernier and Dorre Islands.

Efforts to reintroduce the species to Dirk Hartog in 1977, after the population on that island vanished around 1920, have met with uncertain success. However, populations on the other two islands appear, for the moment at least, to be reasonably secure.

Its preferred habitat is tall scrub within which it shelters by day, often in small groups. At night they move out into adjacent spinifex grasslands on coastal dunes to eat spinifex, other grasses and a variety of shrubs.

Births commonly occur from February to August. A wide variety of predators result in high juvenile mortality. Surviving young achieve independence by six months but commonly do not begin to produce until they are two years old.

The danger of fires on their islands, as well as competition with goats on Bernier Island, are severe threats to their future.

REFERENCES

Burbidge, A.A. and George, A.S., 1978. The flora and fauna of Dirk Hartog Island, Western Australia. *J. Proc. Roy. Soc. West. Aust.* 60:71–90.

Hughes, R.D., 1965. On the age composition of a small sample of individuals from a population of the Banded Hare-wallaby, *Lagostrophus fasciatus* (Peron & Lesueur). *Aust. J. Zool.* 13:75–95.

Ride, W.D.L. and Tyndale-Biscoe, C.H., 1962. Mammals. *In* "The results of an expedition to Bernier and Dorre Islands, Shark Bay, Western Australia in 1959" ed by A.J. Fraser. *West. Aust. Fisheries Dept. Fauna Bull.* 2:54–97.

Thomas O., 1887. On the wallaby commonly known as *Lagorchestes fasciatus. Proc. Zool. Soc. Lond.* 1887:544–47.

RUFOUS HARE-WALLABY

Lagorchestes hirsutus

STATUS: VULNERABLE

SIZE

Nose-vent: *M* 33.0cm (31.0–36.0); *F* 37.5cm (36.0–39.0)
Tail-vent: *M* 27.0cm (26.0–28.0); *F* 27.5cm (24.5–30.5)
Hindfoot (s.u.): *M* 11.7cm; *F* 11.2cm
Ear (n.): *M* 4.0cm; *F* 4.4cm
Adult weight: *M* 1.6kg (1.3–1.8); *F* 1.7kg (0.8–2.0)

This somewhat shaggy-looking hare-wallaby is also one of the rarest. It was once widespread in the deserts of the western half of the continent. But for reasons unknown, possibly as recently as the 1940s and 1950s, it began to radically decline. Now, the only known populations occur in the Tanami Desert of the Northern Territory and on Bernier and Dorre Islands in Western Australia.

The populations on Bernier and Dorre Islands seem to fluctuate markedly in size over short periods of time and the only two colonies known from the Tanami Desert have been estimated (in 1978) to have as few as six to ten individuals each. Clearly, this is a species whose future is anything but secure.

Its habitat preference seems to be for spinifex-sand ridge country. It appears to be well-adapted to frequent and hence less severe bushfires because while it prefers to reside in unburnt stands of spinifex, it seems to prefer to forage for succulent regrowth in adjacent burnt areas. Frequent fires started by lightning or Aborigines were a common feature in central Australia. Now, there are less frequent but more severe fires which may be critical in the range contraction of the species.

Preferred foods appear to include spinifex seeds, sedges and perennial shrubs.

They can and do dig short burrows (up to 70cm) for security or for shelter if the day temperatures become too hot. Otherwise they commonly spend the day hidden under a hummock of spinifex.

REFERENCES

Bolton, B.L. and Latz, P.K., 1978. The Western Hare-wallaby, *Lagorchestes hirsutus* (Gould) (Macropodidae), in the Tanami Desert. *Aust. Wildl. Res.* 5:285–93.

Finlayson, H.H., 1936. "The red centre." Angus and Robertson: Sydney.

Finlayson, H.H., 1961. On central Australian mammals. Part IV. The distribution and status of central Australian species. *Rec. S. Aust. Mus.* 14:141–91.

Ride, W.D.L. and Tyndale-Biscoe, C.H., 1962. Mammals. Pp 54–97 *in* "The results of an expedition to Bernier and Dorre Islands, Shark Bay, Western Australia in 1959" ed by A.J. Frazer. *West. Aust. Fisheries Dept. Fauna Bull.* 2:54–97.

EASTERN HARE-WALLABY

Lagorchestes leporides

STATUS: EXTINCT

SIZE

Nose-vent: *M* 45.0cm; *F* 49.0cm
Tail-vent: *M* 32.0cm; *F* 30.0cm
Hindfoot (s.u.): *M* 12.8cm; *F* 12.2cm
Ear (n.): *M* 4.5cm; *F* 5.7cm

Hare-wallabies as a group received this name from the early European colonists because of their behaviour. Their tendancy to remain motionless under bushes or in grass until virtually stepped on and then their sudden and incredibly fast burst of speed in escaping, reminded the early settlers of the similar behaviour of hares.

This particular species was one of the early victims of the European invasion of the continent. Its demise may have been as much a result of the damage to its habitat caused by cattle and sheep as it was due to the onslaught caused by introduced predators and the inevitable competition for space and food that followed the spread of the rabbit.

It was known to feed at night mainly on grasses and herbs and to spend the day in a nest or "seat" of grass, much as do hares. When caught, they often became quite tame and fed on bread, boiled rice and even biscuits.

They were noted for their extraordinary jumping ability, one individual having leaped straight over the head of its pursuer (John Gould). Another was said by Gerrard Krefft to have leaped as high as 1.8 metres.

REFERENCES
Gould J., 1863. "The mammals of Australia". The author:London.
Jones, F.W., 1924. "The mammals of South Australia. Part II.
Containing the bandicoots and the herbivorous marsupials." Govt. Printer:Adelaide.
Ride, W.D.L., 1970. "A guide to the native mammals of Australia." Oxford Univ. Press:Melbourne.
Ride, W.D.L., 1974. Hare-wallabies. *Aust. Wildl.* 4:1869–71.

SPECTACLED HARE-WALLABY

Lagorchestes conspicillatus

STATUS: SECURE

SIZE

Nose-vent: *M* 48.0cm; *F* 50.5cm (49.0–52.0)
Tail-vent: *M* 42.5cm; *F* 46.0cm
Hindfoot (s.u.): *M* 12.5cm (10.8–13.5); *F* 13.3cm (12.5–14.0)
Ear (n.): *M* 3.3cm (3.2–3.3); *F* 3.7cm (3.5–3.9)
Adult weight: *M* and *F* 1.6–4.5kg

This widespread hare-wallaby is the only one that has not suffered major range reduction since Europeans arrived. It is reasonably widespread in Queensland and common in some open forest areas of the east coast. In the Northern Territory they vanished from areas of dense *Acacia* thickets along the central ranges but are still secure in the northern part of the state. In Western Australia they are rare except on Barrow Island and they may have vanished from most if not all of the Pilbara Region.

In the preferred habitats of open forest, *Acacia* thickets, open savannah woodlands and spinifex grasslands, they apparently browse or graze on shrubs and the tips of spinifex (*Triodia*) leaves.

Nests with a female and young have been found in thick tussocks of spinifex. Other individuals have been found resting by day in simple depressions under shrubs.

Breeding occurs in all months but most young are born in March and September. Pouch-life lasts for about 150 days and the young reach sexual maturity at the end of their first year.

Although they will growl and are very aggressive if captured, when released they commonly hop a few metres away and placidly resume feeding. If they are accidentally encountered in a nest, they may not move until the nest is actually trodden on at which moment they will bolt out from underfoot.

REFERENCES

Burbidge, A.A. and Main, A.R., 1971. Report on a visit of inspection to Barrow Island, November 1969. *Dept. Fisheries and Fauna West. Aust. Rept.* No. 8.

Butler, W.H., 1970. A summary of the vertebrate fauna of Barrow Island, Western Australia. *West. Aust. Nat.* 11:149–60.

Dawson, W.R. and Bennett, A.F., 1971. Thermoregulation in the marsupial *Lagorchestes conspicillatus. J. Physiol.* 63:239–41.

Parker, S.A., 1973. An annotated checklist of the native land mammals of the Northern Territory. *Rec. S. Aust. Mus.* 16:1–57.

REMOTE DESERT HABITAT OF THE CENTRAL HARE-WALLABY.

CENTRAL HARE-WALLABY

Lagorchestes asomatus

STATUS: EXTINCT

SIZE

Unknown, but the size of the skull suggests that it was the smallest species of the genus.

Our knowledge of this species is a model of frustration. The single known individual was collected by Michael Terry in August, 1932, somewhere between Mount Farewell and Lake McKay in the Northern Territory.

Unfortunately, he saved nothing except the skull and lower jaws. The fresh carcass was, tragically, discarded and he recorded no notes specifically referable to this animal.

Terry's description of the habitat near the collection site was of sandhills from one horizon to the other. Considering the relatively recent date of collection which is well after the introduction of most of the noxious mammals that established in that country, and the relatively remote desert area, there is at least a small chance that this hare-wallaby still survives.

Features of the skull suggest that this rarest of the kangaroos was probably more closely related to the Spectacled Hare-wallaby than to any of the other species. Its enormous middle ear region suggests that it may have been well-suited to detecting the low-frequency sounds associated with striking owls or snakes.

REFERENCES

Aitken, P.F., 1983. Central Hare-wallaby. P200 *in* "The Australian Museum complete book of Australian mammals" ed by R. Strahan. Angus and Robertson:Sydney.

Finlayson, H.H., 1943. A new species of *Lagorchestes* (Marsupialia). *Trans. R. Soc. S. Aust.* 67:319–21.

Parker, S.A., 1973. An annotated checklist of the native land mammals of the Northern Territory. *Rec. S. Aust. Mus.* 16:1–57.

CRESCENT NAILTAIL WALLABY

Onychogalea lunata

STATUS: EXTINCT

SIZE

Nose-vent: *M* and *F* 37.1–50.8cm
Tail-vent: *M* and *F* 15.3–33.0cm
Hindfoot (s.u.): *M* 12.0cm
Ear (n.): *M* 5.8cm

This once widespread species is the worst casualty among nailtail wallabies, the last one having been seen in 1964 as a fox-ravaged carcass near the Warburton Range of Western Australia.

John Gould referred to this rabbit-sized species as similar to the Northern Nailtail Wallaby but "... certainly less ornamental ...". Being inconspicuous does not, however, seem to have given it much advantage in the business of survival. It was described as being fond of sunning itself in the open glades between its refuges of thick scrub and dense thickets. In these open glades, dogs often succeeded in bailing them up in hollow logs.

One early naturalist recorded that when chased by dogs they would sometimes make for a hole in the base of a hollow tree and, upon entering, clamber up the inside of the tree.

They are not known to have made nests. Instead, they waited out the heat of the day living in hollows which they dug in the soft earth beneath a bush.

REFERENCES
Finlayson, H.H., 1961. On central Australian mammals Part IV –
The distribution and status of central Australian species. *Rec. S. Aust. Mus.* 14:141–91.
Jones, F.W. 1924. "The mammals of South Australia. Part II.
Containing the bandicoots and the herbivorous marsupials". Govt. Printer:Adelaide.
Parker, S.A., 1973. An annotated checklist of the native land mammals
of the Northern Territory. *Rec. S. Aust. Mus.* 16:1-57.
Ride, W.D.L., 1970. "A guide to the native mammals of Australia". Oxford University Press:Melbourne.

BRIDLED NAILTAIL WALLABY

Onychogalea fraenata

STATUS: ENDANGERED

SIZE

Nose-vent: *M* 51.0–100.0cm; *F* 43.0–82.5cm
Tail-vent: *M* 38.0–54.0cm; *F* 36.0–44.0cm
Hindfoot (s.u.): *M* 16.0cm; *F* 12.2cm
Ear (n.): *M* 8.9cm; *F* 8.3cm
Adult weight: *M* 5–6kg; *F* 4–5kg

This elegant nailtail wallaby was stated in 1863 to be common throughout the Darling Downs and other areas of eastern Queensland where it persisted apparently until the 1930s. It was also common in New South Wales until it vanished in the 1920s. And, although it was regarded in 1857 to be the most common wallaby in the mallee scrub of Western Victoria, by the early part of the 20th century it was extinct in the state. As a result, as recently as 1970, the species as a whole was regarded to be probably extinct.

Then, in 1973, a population was discovered and recognized by a local fencer working near Dingo in eastern Queensland. Dr Greg Gordon of the Queensland National Parks and Wildlife Service subsequently located populations in the region covering a total area of about 11,240 hectares.

Preferred habitats appear to include semi-arid savannah scrubland and woodlands dominated by Brigalow (*Acacia harpophyla*) or other species of *Acacia*.

Females are said to commonly but not always give birth in May, and one individual lived in captivity for five years and six months. Very little else is known about the life cycle of this rare wallaby.

REFERENCES

Gordon, G. and Lawrie, B.C., 1980. The rediscovery of the Bridled Nailtail Wallaby
(*Onychogalea fraenata* Gould) in Queensland. *Aust. Wildl. Res.* 7:339–45.
Nelson, J., 1974. Nail-tails and scaly-tails. *Aust. Wildl.* 3: 1226–29.

Northern Nailtail Wallaby

Onychogalea unguifera

STATUS: SECURE

SIZE

Nose-vent: *M* 60.0cm (54.0–69.0); *F* 57.0cm (49.0–60.0)
Tail-vent: *M* 66.0cm (60.0–73.0); *F* 63.0cm (60.0–65.0)
Hindfoot (s.u.): *F* 29.0cm
Ear (n.): *F* 6.4cm
Adult weight: *M* 7.5kg (6.0–9.0); *F* 5.8kg (4.5–7.0)

This species is the largest and, in the face of human adversity, the most successful. It continues to occupy almost the whole of the range it was originally found in by the early settlers of northern Australia.

Its preferred habitats include timbered or lightly-wooded floodplains, shrub-savannah and savannah woodlands. Here they feed on grass-roots and *Melaleuca* leaves during the dry season and green grasses in the wet season.

All nailtail wallabies have a curious horny spur on the tip of their tails, much as do lions and bilbies. Although the function of this structure is unknown, it has been speculated that they use it when running, as a "steering" aid to effect rapid directional shifts, the tip presumably being jabbed into the ground in the opposite direction of the intended turn. This idea, although imaginative, seems unlikely because when running they normally hold their tails curved upwards with the tip pointing skywards.

For their size, they are very strong wallabies and it seems improbable that any predator smaller than a fox would be a bother to them. Graziers, dingoes, pythons and foxes are, however, plentiful within their range.

REFERENCES

Dahl, K., 1897. Biological notes on North-Australian Mammalia. *The Zoologist. Series 4. Vol.* 1:189–216.

Nelson, J., 1974. Nail-tails and scaly-tails. *Aust. Wildl.* 3:1226–29.

Parker, S.A., 1973. An annotated checklist of the native land mammals of the Northern Territory. *Rec. S. Aust. Mus.* 16:1–57.

BENNETT'S TREE-KANGAROO

Dendrolagus bennettianus

STATUS: VULNERABLE

SIZE

Nose-vent: *M* 63.5cm (62.0–65.0); *F* 50.0–61.0cm
Tail-vent: *M* 85.0cm (75.0–94.0); *F* 63.1–68.5cm
Hindfoot (s.u.): *M* 13.0cm
Ear (n.): 3.8cm
Adult weight: *M* 13.0kg

Bennett's Tree-Kangaroo was formerly known 120km south of its present southern limit (the Daintree River). The reasons for the range reduction are not known, but logging as well as hunting have no doubt contributed to the stresses facing this kangaroo.

This species is less well-known than Lumholtz's Tree-kangaroo, but appears to be broadly similar in biology. It has been seen feeding on creepers, bird-nest ferns, the leaves of white cedar and other trees, and most types of wild fruits.

Young reportedly leave the pouch around August. Apart from this tidbit, nothing else is known about its life history.

In captivity they are sometimes very aggressive. Males often fight with each other and, in some instances, this has led to the death of weaker individuals. In the wild, fights rarely lead to death because the loser can retreat, an option unavailable to captives.

Although commonly an inhabitant of the crowns of the rainforest trees, they have frequently been observed travelling along open ground at some distance from the nearest forest. Aerial leaps of six to nine metres have been observed while they are moving from tree to tree.

On occasions when they abandon the tree tops for the ground, vertical leaps to the ground of up to 18 metres have been recorded.

REFERENCES

De Vis, C.W., 1887. Notice of a probable new species of *Dendrolagus. Proc. R. Soc. Qd* 3:11–14.
Groves, C.P., 1982. The systematics of tree kangaroos (*Dendrolagus:* Marsupialia, Macropodidae). *Aust. Mammal.* 5:157–86.
Rothschild, L. and Dollman, G., 1936. The genus *Dendrolagus. Trans. Zool. Soc. Lond.* 21:477–548.
Waite, E.R., 1894. Observations on *Dendrolagus bennettianus*, De Vis. *Trans. R. Soc. S. Aust.* 18:571–82.

LUMHOLTZ'S TREE-KANGAROO

Dendrolagus lumholtzi

STATUS: VULNERABLE

SIZE

Nose-vent: *M* 55.5cm (52.0–59.0); *F* 54.8cm (50.0–60.0)
Tail-vent: *M* 66.8cm (60.0–73.6); *F* 67.6cm (64.0–70.5)
Hindfoot (s.u.): *M* 13.0cm; *F* 12.6cm (11.8–13.5)
Ear (n.): *M* 4.5cm; *F* 4.9cm (4.1–5.6)
Adult weight: *M* 7.4kg (3.7–10.0); *F* 5.9kg (5.2–7.0)

The reason for regarding this extraordinary kangaroo to be "vulnerable" is its tendency to occur in isolated patches of remnant rainforest, situations that are not easily recolonized if disasters such as disease overtake the animals of a particular patch. However, in some areas of its limited range, it is in fact common.

When first seen in the highland rainforests by Europeans, these tree-climbing and seemingly unkangaroo-like kangaroos were sometimes mistaken for monkeys. Although they can and do hop, they can also walk along branches quadrupedally like non-hopping animals. Perhaps even more of a surprise is their observed ability to climb a hanging rope. Extraordinary leaps of 18 metres out of trees to the ground have also been observed.

Most of the daytime is spent curled up like a ball in the tops of tall trees. The hair of their backs is directed away in all directions from the shoulder region so that, when rain falls on them while they are sleeping, it probably runs off without wetting them.

Foods include leaves, strips of bark, fruits and probably small animals when they can catch them. In captivity they have been known to consume raw meat.

REFERENCES

Cairn, E.J. and Grant, R., 1890. Report on a collecting trip to northeastern Queensland during April to September, 1889. *Rec. Aust. Mus.* 1:27–31.

Collett, R., 1884. On some apparently new marsupials from Queensland. *Proc. Zool. Soc. Lond.* 26:381–88.

Groves, C.P., 1982. The systematics of tree kangaroos (*Dendrolagus*; Marsupialia, Macropodidae). *Aust. Mammal.* 5:157–86.

Johnston, T.H. and Gillies, C.D., 1918. Notes on records of tree kangaroos in Queensland. *Aust. Zool.* 1:153–56.

Rothschild, L. and Dollman, G., 1936. The genus *Dendrolagus. Trans. Zool. Soc. Lond.* 21:477–548.

Windsor, D.E. and Dagg, A.I., 1971. The gaits of the Macropodidae (Marsupialia). *J. Zool. Lond.* 16:165–75.

RED-NECKED PADEMELON

Thylogale thetis

STATUS: SECURE

SIZE

Nose-vent: *M* 52.0cm (30.0–62.0); *F* 42.0cm (29.0–50.0)
Tail-vent: *M* 43.0cm (27.0–51.0); *F* 33.3cm (27.0–39.5)
Hindfoot (s.u.): *M* 12.6cm (11.1–13.8); *F* 12.1cm (12.0–12.2)
Ear (n.): *M* 6.6cm (5.7–7.2); *F* 5.8cm(5.5–6.1)
Adult weight: *M* 7.0kg (2.5–9.1); *F* 3.8kg (1.8–4.3)

This species appears to be in no danger. In fact it is one of the commonest rainforest mammals in southeastern Queensland and northeastern New South Wales. Feeding aggregations have been seen that numbered as high as 57 individuals per half hectare. This abundance was noted as early as 1863 by John Gould who suggested it was one of the best-known of the wallabies and, because of their "tender and well-flavoured" flesh, was said by Gould to be valued by the settlers as well as Aborigines.

Preferred habitats are rainforest and wet sclerophyll forests but they are most frequently seen at night on the adjacent grassed clearings.

Foods known to be eaten include grasses, browse including tree-seedlings, fruits, wild tobacco and even insects.

Recent radio-tracking studies revealed that they rarely move more than 70 metres out into pasture adjacent to rainforest or (in this study) more than 500 metres back into the rainforest. They were not nocturnal within the forest but, instead, travelled by day in search of food and clearings in which to bask in the sun. This use of pastures by night and forests by day may be a strategy to reduce predation.

REFERENCES

Johnson, K.A., 1977. "Ecology and management of the Red-necked Pademelon, *Thylogale thetis*, on the Dorrigo Plateau of northern New South Wales". Ph.D. thesis: University of New England, Armidale.

Johnson, K.A., 1980. Spatial and temporal use of habitat by the Red-necked Pademelon, *Thylogale thetis* (Marsupialia:Macropodidae). *Aust. Wildl. Res.* 7:157–66.

Troughton, E. LeG., 1951. The kangaroo family. The pademelons or scrub-wallabies–1. *Aust. Mus. Mag.* 10:218–22.

THE TASMANIAN PADEMELON

Thylogale billardierii

STATUS: SECURE

SIZE

Nose-vent: *M* 63.0cm; *F* 56.0cm
Tail-vent: M 41.7cm (34.5–48.3); *F* 32.0cm
Hindfoot (s.u.): 14.0cm
Ear (n.): 6.5cm (6.4–6.5)
Adult weight: *M* 7.0kg (3.8-12.0); *F* 3.9kg (2.4–10.0)

John Gould commented in 1863 that he had " . . . little doubt that the habitat of this Wallaby is limited to Van Diemen's Land and the larger islands in Bass Straight, in all of which localities it is so numerous that the thousands annually destroyed make no apparent diminution of its numbers". He was right in perpetuity about the last remark but briefly wrong about the first.

These pademelons are still regularly culled in large numbers seemingly without any detrimental long-term affects. However, although the same species was in fact discovered on the mainland not long after Gould published, European activity soon pushed it over the brink. The last mainland individual vanished before the turn of the century turning Gould's error into reality.

This species is a seasonal breeder. Most young are born in April, May and June. The gestation period is 30.2 days. At birth the young weigh 0.4gm, have a head of 0.7cm long, a hindfoot 0.3cm long and a 0.5cm tail. The eyes open at about 120 days and hair develops at about 140 days. The young stay in the pouch for about 200 days and become sexually mature at about 14 to 15 months.

Foods include grasses, herbs and browse.

REFERENCES

Morton, S.R. and Burton, T.C., 1973. Observations on the behaviour of the macropodid marsupial *Thylogale billardieri* (Desmarest) in captivity. *Aust. Zool.* 18:1–14.

Rose, R.W. and McCartney, D.J., 1982. Reproduction of the Red-bellied Pademelon, *Thylogale billardierii* (Marsupialia). *Aust. Wildl. Res.* 9:27–32.

Rose, R.W. and McCartney, D.J., 1982. Growth of the Red-bellied Pademelon, *Thylogale billardierii*, and age estimation of pouch young. *Aust. Wildl. Res.* 9:33–38.

THE QUOKKA

Setonix brachyurus

STATUS: VULNERABLE

SIZE

Nose-vent: *M* 48.7cm (43.5–54.0); *F* 46.8cm (40.0–50.0)
Tail-vent: *M* 28.9cm (26.0–31.0); *F* 26.5cm (24.5–28.5)
Hindfoot (s.u.): *F* 10.1cm
Ear (n.): *M F* 4.3cm
Adult weight: *M* 3.6kg (2.7–4.2); *F* 2.9kg (2.7–3.5)

John Gilbert, who collected mammals for the naturalist John Gould, noted that the "Quak-a", as the Aborigines in Western Australia called the animal, was abundant in all swampy areas that skirted the coast of southwestern Western Australia and was destroyed in "great numbers" for food. When wanting to procure Quokkas they evidently fired the bush from one side and then waited with spears in a clearing on the other side.

Today, the Quokka is generally rare on the mainland but survives in reasonable numbers on Bald and Rottnest Islands. Rottnest Island was so named in 1696 by the Dutch navigator Willem de Vlamingh because he mistook the abundant Quokkas for large rats.

On Rottnest Island these small kangaroos have a short breeding season which starts in January (with births from February) if the season is mild, but in March if it is hot. The gestation period is about 27 days. Like most kangaroos, the female mates again the day after giving birth. This second embryo then develops until it is about the size of a pinhead and made up of only about 100 cells. At this point its development stops unless the first young is prematurely lost from the pouch. If this happens, development of the second young resumes and the second young is born. Pouch life lasts about 6 months and sexual maturity is achieved by the end of the second year.

REFERENCES

Kitchener, D.J., 1981. Factors influencing selection of shelter by individual Quokkas, *Setonix brachyurus* (Marsupialia), during hot summer days on Rottnest Island. *Aust. J. Zool.* 29:75–84.

Packer, W.C., 1969. Observations on the behaviour of the marsupial *Setonix brachyurus* (Quoy & Gaimard) in an enclosure. *J. Mammal.* 50:8–20.

Storr, G.M., 1964. Studies on marsupial nutrition IV. Diet of the Quokka, *Setonix brachyurus* (Quoy & Gaimard), on Rottnest Island, Western Australia. *Aust. J. Biol. Sci.* 17:469-81.

Tyndale-Biscoe, H., 1973. "Life of marsupials". Edward Arnold:London.

UNADORNED ROCK-WALLABY

Petrogale inornata

STATUS: SECURE

SIZE

Nose-vent: *M* 52.3cm (51.0–55.0); *F* 52.4cm (49.8–55.0)
Tail-vent: *M* 54.7cm (51.0–59.5); *F* 53.4cm (51.2–55.4)
Hindfoot (s.u.): *M* 15.2cm (14.5–15.7); *F* 14.2cm (14.1–14.3)
Ear (n.): *M* 6.1cm (5.9–6.3); *F* 6.0cm (5.9–6.1)
Adult weight: *M* 4.9kg (4.5–5.5); *F* 4.5kg (4.2–5.0)

John Gould commented in 1863 that this " . . . plain-coloured but rare species is one I would recommend to the notice of the naturalists and explorers who may visit the north coast of Australia, where it was discovered by Mr Bynoe". It is in fact still available in northeastern Queensland for interested naturalists.

This species is one of several in northern Queensland about which very little is known. In captivity, births have occurred in all months. The gestation period is 30 to 32 days and the young leave the pouch by about 227 days.

There are at least five different varieties of Unadorned Rock-wallabies. One of these, *Petrogale inornata assimilis*, occurs only on Great Palm Island and Magnetic Island as well as the adjacent mainland. It is probable that when sea-levels were lower during the Pleistocene Epoch (the "Ice Ages"), these islands were joined to the mainland. When the ice melted sea level rose and the islands and their rock-wallabies became isolated.

REFERENCES

Johnson, P.M., 1979. Reproduction in the Plain Rock-wallaby *Petrogale penicillata inornata* Gould, in captivity, with age estimation of the pouch young. *Aust. Wildl. Res.* 6:1–4.

Maynes, G.M., 1982. A new species of rock wallaby, *Petrogale persephone* (Marsupialia:Macropodidae), from Proserpine central Queensland. *Aust. Mammal.* 5:47–58.

Thomas, O., 1926. On various mammals obtained during Capt. Wilkins's expedition in Australia. *Ann. Mag. Nat. Hist. Ser. 9* 17:625–35.

Proserpine Rock-wallaby

Petrogale persephone

STATUS: ENDANGERED

SIZE

Nose-vent: *M* 52.3cm (51.0–55.0); *F* 52.4cm (49.8–55.0)
Tail-vent: *M* 54.7cm (51.0–59.5); *F* 53.4cm (51.2–55.4)
Hindfoot (s.u.): *M* 15.2cm (14.5–15.7); *F* 14.2cm (14.1–14.3)
Ear (n.): *M* 6.1cm (5.9–6.3); *F* 6.0cm (5.9–6.1)
Adult weight: *M* 5.5kg (4.5–8.0); *F* 4.5kg (4.2–5.0)

This newly-named species came to the attention of mammalogists only as recently as 1976. Gerry Maynes commented in 1982 that it was " . . . remarkable that such a large species of mammal could remain unknown to science until now, especially as the Proserpine district is not a remote unsettled region". Although the Proserpine branch of the Wildlife Preservation Society of Queensland knew about its existence, the first specimen was not collected until 1976.

It is probable that its rainforest habitat and very restricted distribution have contributed to keeping it a mystery for so long. But now that it is no longer a mystery, it is the focus of concerned conservationists. It is known from only two localities in the Proserpine district. The reasons for its decline may be related to the apparent increase in range of the adjacent Unadorned Rock-wallaby.

Like all rock-wallabies, it lives among rocky outcrops but feeds on grasses in the nearby open sclerophyll forest that surrounds the rainforest. When threatened, they have been observed to climb up trees.

Curiously, the closest relative of this rainforest rock-wallaby appears to be the strikingly-coloured Yellow-footed Rock-wallaby of arid Queensland, New South Wales and South Australia.

REFERENCES

Maynes, G.M., 1982. A new species of rock wallaby, *Petrogale persephone* (Marsupialia:Macropodidae), from Proserpine central Queensland. *Aust. Mammal.* 5:47–58.

The Nabarlek

Petrogale concinna

STATUS: VULNERABLE

SIZE

Nose-vent: *M* 26.8cm (20.5–33.7); *F* 31.2cm (30.8–31.5)
Tail-vent: *M* 29.1cm (23.1–34.5); *F* 31.6cm (31.4–31.8)
Hindfoot (s.u.): *M* 9.0cm (7.0–10.0); *F* 9.2cm (9.1–9.3)
Ear (n.): *M* and *F* 4.3cm (4.1–4.5)
Adult weight: *M* and *F* 1.4kg (1.1–1.7)

The Norwegian zoologist Knut Dahl was obviously impressed by the "Bolwak", as the local Aborigines called this diminitive rock-wallaby, when he wrote in 1897: "Deep in the caverns and crevices amongst the colossal granite boulders, where the rays of the sun never reach the little wary "Bolwak" spends the day, sleeping lightly . . . Their speed and dexterity is simply marvellous, and seeing one of these little wallabies running through the broken country, one might almost imagine it to be the shadow of a bird flying swiftly overhead".

No less remarkable are aspects of the Nabarlek's cuisine. Although in the wet season it feeds on grasses, during the dry season it seeks out *Marsilea crenata*, a fern that may contain as much as 26 per cent (dry weight) silica, an extremely abrasive substance used by these plants in part to avoid being eaten by animals such as hungry kangaroos. Possibly as an evolutionary response to the severe tooth wear caused by this diet, the Nabarlek is the only kangaroo that can produce an unlimited number of replacement teeth.

This rock-wallaby appears to be able to breed throughout the year although most young have been observed in the wet season. The gestation period is about 31 days. Pouch life lasts about 180 days and individuals become sexually mature during their second year.

REFERENCES

Briscoe, D.A., Calaby, J.H., Close, R.L., Maynes, G.M., Murtagh, C.E. and Sharman, G.B., 1982. Isolation, introgression and genetic variation in rock-wallabies. Pp73–87 *in* "Species at risk: research in Australia" ed by R.H. Groves and W.D.L. Ride. Australian Academy of Science:Canberra.

Dahl, K., 1897. Biological notes on north-Australian Mammalia. *The Zoologist* No. 671:189–216.

Sanson, G.D., 1983. Nabarlek *Peradorcas concinna*. P223 *in* "The Australian Museum complete book of Australian mammals" ed by R. Strahan. Angus and Robertson:Sydney.

Thomas, O., 1904. On a collection of mammals made by Mr. J.T. Tunney in Arnhem Land, Northern Territory of South Australia. *Nov. Zool.* 11:222–29.

THE PRINCE REGENT RIVER RESERVE, ONE OF THE FEW KNOWN HABITATS OF THE WARABE.

WARABI

Petrogale burbidgei

STATUS: SECURE

SIZE

Nose-vent: *M* 32.4cm (30.9–35.3); *F* 30.0cm (21.8–32.8)
Tail-vent: *M* 27.6cm (29.9–33.0); *F* 23.3cm (25.2–32.2)
Hindfoot (s.u.): *M* 8.6cm (8.2–9.2); *F* 8.9cm (7.7–9.5)
Ear (n.): *M* 3.2cm (3.0–3.3); *F* 3.3cm (2.9–3.6)
Adult weight: *M* 1.2kg (1.0–1.4); *F* 1.1kg (1.2–1.4)

This smallest of the rock-wallabies is so far known only from the Mitchell Plateau, Prince Regent River Reserve and several islands (e.g., Bigge Island) of the Bonaparte Archipelago in the Kimberley Region of Western Australia. In these remote areas it avoided detection until 1963 and was described only as recently as 1978.

Although it appears to prefer low woodlands with the grassey understory on fractured sandstone terrain, it has also been seen on rugged sandstone cliffs.

Apart from the fact that pouch young have been found with individuals collected in June, August and October to November, very little else is known about its reproductive biology.

REFERENCES

Kitchener, D.J. and Sanson, G., 1978. *Petrogale burbidgei* (Marsupialia, Macropodidae), a new rock wallaby from Kimberley, Western Australia. *Rec. West. Aust. Mus.* 6:269–85.

ROTHSCHILD'S ROCK-WALLABY

Petrogale rothschildi

STATUS: SECURE

SIZE

Nose-vent: *M* and *F* 52.5cm (43.0–58.0)
Tail-vent: *M* and *F* 59.0cm (47.0–67.0)
Hindfoot (s.u.): *M* 14.5cm
Ear (n.): *M* 5.6cm
Adult weight: 5.3kg

This species is one of the most poorly-known of the genus. Its stronghold is the igneous rocks of the Hamersley Range area in Western Australia but it also occurs on Enderby and Rosemary Islands in the Dampier Archipelago. A population that occurred on Lewis Island may now be extinct. These island rock-wallabies appear to be dwarf forms of the mainland species.

In a study by E.H.M. Ealey into the use of rock piles on Woodstock Station by these rock-wallabies and other animals, he found that in the deep crevasses and caves between the rocks, air temperatures remained between 27° and 32°C while outside temperatures in the shade ranged from 18° to 46°.

Clearly animals that stayed in the caves by day were much less heat-stressed and hence probably required less water than animals that spent the day resting in the shade of a tree.

REFERENCES
Maynes, G.M. and Sharman, G.B., 1983. Rothschild's Rock-wallaby *Petrogale rothschildi*. P216 *in*
"The Australian Museum complete book of Australian mammals" ed by R. Strahan. Angus and Robertson:Sydney.
Ride, W.D.L., 1970. "A guide to the native mammals of Australia". Oxford University Press:Melbourne.

GODMAN'S ROCK-WALLABY

Petrogale godmani

STATUS: VULNERABLE

SIZE

Nose-vent: *M* and *F* 49.5cm (45.5–52.5)
Tail-vent: *M* and *F* 55.1cm (48.0–59.2)
Hindfoot (s.u.): *M* 14.0cm
Ear (n.): *M* 5.9cm
Adult weight: 5.0kg

When the prolific taxonomist Oldfield Thomas described this new species in 1923 he was said to have "... expressed his pleasure at being able to bring forward so fine a discovery as one of the first-fruits of the Godman Exploration Fund, which has been recently founded by Dame Alice Godman in memory of her husband, Dr. R. Ducane Godman, S.F.R., the well-known naturalist".

Private benefactors such as Dame Alice Godman were crucial in enabling early zoologists to discover many of the then unknown species of Australian mammals. This type of support is still vitally needed to permit discovery to continue, particularly in the remote and largely unexamined areas of northern Australia and New Guinea.

Very little is known about the biology of Godman's Rock-wallaby. It is reasonably widespread in far northeastern Queensland and occurs in rocky areas in habitats ranging from open forests with grassy understories to rainforest.

There appear to be two types, the typical form from near Cooktown and a Cape York race which occurs north of Coen.

The species is considered vulnerable because its range appears to be contracting at the expense of a northward increase in the range of the Unadorned Rock-wallaby.

REFERENCES

Maynes, G.M. and Sharman, G.B., 1983. Godman's Rock-wallaby *Petrogale godmani*. P215 *in* "The Australian Museum complete book of Australian mammals" ed by R. Strahan. Angus and Robertson: Sydney.

Thomas, O., 1923. A new rock-kangaroo (*Petrogale*) which had been obtained in northern Queensland by Mr. T. Sherrin. . . . Proc. Zool. Soc. Lond. 1923:177–78.

SHORT-EARED ROCK-WALLABY

Petrogale brachyotis

STATUS: SECURE

SIZE

Nose-vent: *M* 46.7cm (40.0–51.0); *F* 42.0cm (38.0–46.0)
Tail-vent: *M* 41.5cm (34.0–49.0); *F* 39.8cm (34.5–45.0)
Hindfoot (s.u.): *M* 12.7cm (11.3–14.0); *F* 11.1cm (10.2–12.0)
Ear (n.): *M* 5.6cm(4.7-6.5); *F* 3.8cm (3.5–4.1)
Adult weight: *M* 4.2kg

There are at least four distinctive types of the Short-eared Rock-wallaby: the first-known *brachyotis* type from the Kimberleys; a Victoria River race from the Northern Territory; an Arnhem Land race (which has variously been called *signata, venstula, wilkinsi* and *longmani*); and a larger unnamed form that occurs geographically between the last two types. When more extensive studies are carried out on the species, it is possible that one or more of these forms may prove to be distinctive species. At present, however, they are regarded to be races of a single species.

Like other rock-wallabies, this species is restricted to rocky outcrops with fissures, ledges or caves. Around Oenpelli in the Northern Territory they were observed to be active by day as well as night. Pouch young have been observed in October.

Last century, George Grey described this species as " . . . excessively wild and shy in its habits, frequenting in the day-time the highest and most inaccessible rocks, and only coming down to the valleys to feed early in the morning and late in the evening. When disturbed in the day-time it bounds among the roughest and most precipitous rocks, apparently with the greatest facility, and is so watchful and wary that it is by no means easy to get a shot at it".

REFERENCES

Johnson, D.H., 1964. Mammals of the Arnhem Land Expedition. Pp427–515 *in* "Records of the American-Australian Scientific Expedition to Arnhem Land, 4 (Zoology)" ed by R.L. Specht. Melbourne University Press:Melbourne.

Sharman, G.B. and Maynes, G.M., 1983. Short-eared Rock-wallaby *Petrogale brachyotis*. P221 *in* "The Australian Museum complete book of Australian mammals" ed by R. Strahan. Angus and Robertson:Sydney.

Thomas, O., 1926. Two new rock-wallabies (*Petrogale*) discovered by Capt. G.W. Wilkins in northern Australia. *Ann. Mag. Nat. Hist. Ser. 9* 17:184–87.

Thomas, O., 1926. On various mammals obtained during Capt. Wilkins's expedition in Australia. *Ann Mag. Nat. Hist. Ser. 9* 17:625–35.

BRUSH-TAILED ROCK-WALLABY

Petrogale penicillata

STATUS: SECURE

SIZE

Nose-vent: *M* 51.3cm (49.0–53.5); *F* 49.3cm (47.0–51.5)
Tail-vent: *M* 54.5cm (44.0–65.0); *F* 50.0cm (42.0–58.0)
Hindfoot (s.u.): *M* 14.4cm (12.5–16.2); *F* 13.9cm (12.0–15.7)
Ear (n.): *M* 5.5cm (4.7–6.2); *F* 5.7cm (5.3–6.1)
Adult weight: *M* 5.9kg; *F* 5.0kg

There appear to be two distinctive forms of this rock-wallaby: the typical form from Victoria, New South Wales and the southern border region of Queensland and the slightly smaller and lighter *herberti* form from southeastern Queensland. Of these, only the Victorian populations seem to be endangered although other populations have declined in size. The New South Wales populations, for example, once extended into rocky country well east of the Divide. It has been suggested that its decline and the decline in Victoria were in large part caused by the spread of the European fox soon after settlement.

This rock-wallaby occupies rugged areas commonly in sclerophyll forest, rainforest or even semi-arid savannah woodland. Its diet includes mostly grasses, rather than forbs and browse. In a recent study of habitat preference, it was determined that within rocky areas, sites occupied had twice the number of ledges, three times the number of caves and many more climbable paths from the base of the rocky slopes to the top of the cliff than did adjacent unoccupied sites. Chosen sites also had cliffs or slopes that faced the sun for much of the day.

They normally live in small colonies where individuals may have overlapping home ranges of about 15 hectares each. However, males appear to have larger home ranges than females.

It is also of interest that this species, which was introduced to the island of Oahu in 1916, is now firmly established in Hawaii.

REFERENCES

Finlayson, H.H., 1931. On mammals from the Dawson Valley, Queensland. Part I. *Trans. Proc. R. Soc. S. Aust.* 55:67–89.
Kirkpatrick, T., 1964. Rock wallabies around Warwick. *Wildl. in Australia* 1:32–33.
Lim, L., Robinson, A. and Copley, P., 1981. Rock wallabies genus *Petrogale*. Pp21-26 *in* "Kangaroos and other macropods of New South Wales" ed by C. Haigh. New South Wales National Parks and Wildlife Service:Sydney.
Short, J., 1982. Habitat requirements of the Brush-tailed Rock-wallaby, *Petrogale penicillata*, in New South Wales. *Aust. Wildl. Res.* 9:239–46.
Wakefield, N.A., 1971. The Brush-tailed Rock Wallaby (*Petrogale penicillata*) in western Victoria. *Vict. Nat.* 88:92–102.

BLACK-FOOTED ROCK-WALLABY

Petrogale lateralis

STATUS: VULNERABLE

SIZE

Nose-vent: *M* 49.9cm (49.8–50.0); *F* 53.5cm (46.5–67.1)
Tail-vent: *F* 48.0cm (45.0–51.0)
Hindfoot (s.u.): *M* 13.6cm; *F* 14.0cm (12.1–15.0)
Ear (n.): M 4.3cm; *F* 5.6cm (5.0–6.2)
Adult weight: *M* 6.4kg (5.0–7.7); *F* 4.6kg (3.5–5.8)

Much about this species has an element of mystery about it. In the first place, there are fair reasons to doubt whether all of the forms placed within this species (i.e., *lateralis, hacketti, purpureicollis*, an unnamed MacDonnell Ranges form and a western Kimberley form) should in fact be placed here. This is particularly true of the MacDonnell Ranges form. Some of these may represent distinct species of their own.

Similarly mysterious is the complete disappearance of the *hacketti* form from the southwestern mainland of Western Australia. It was, according to Gould, very abundant at the time of European settlement in the rocky districts of the Swan River particularly in the Toodyay district.

John Gilbert noted (in Gould's "Mammals of Australia" in 1863) that this was a very shy and wary animal and that while feeding in open patches of grass, it never strayed more than ". . . two or three hundred yards from its rocky retreats". He added that "When alarmed, it leaps most extraordinary distances from rock to rock and point to point with the utmost rapidity . . . the best way to procure specimens is to walk over the rocks without shoes, and station yourself within gunshot distance of the principle entrance to their caverns, when, on making their appearance in the middle of the day for the purpose of sunning themselves, they are easily shot".

Apart from Gilbert's brief remarks and those of a few others, very little else is known about the biology of this species.

REFERENCES

Hornsby, P.E., 1979. Feeding behaviour in the Pearson Island Rock Wallaby. *Vict. Nat.* 96:38–41.

Johnson, D.H., 1964. Mammals. Pp427–515 *in* "Records of the American-Australian Scientific Expedition to Arnhem Land, 4 (Zoology)" ed by R.L. Specht. Melbourne University:Melbourne.

Le Souef, A.S., 1924. Notes on some rock wallabies, genus *Petrogale*, with descriptions of two new species. *Aust. Zool.* 3:272–76.

Merrilees, D., 1979. Prehistoric rock-wallabies (Marsupialia, Macropodidae, *Petrogale*) in the far south-west of Western Australia. *J. Proc. R. Soc. West. Aust.* 61:73–96.

Sharman, G.B. and Maynes G.M., 1983. Black-footed Rock-wallaby Petrogale lateralis Pp209–10 *in* "The Australian Museum complete book of Australian mammals" ed by R. Strahan. Angus and Robertson:Sydney.

YELLOW-FOOTED ROCK-WALLABY

Petrogale xanthopus

STATUS: VULNERABLE

SIZE

Nose-vent: *M* 72.5cm (65.0–80.0); *F* 64.0cm (60.0–68.0)
Tail-vent: *M* 62.5cm (60.0–65.0); *F* 58.3cm (56.5–60.0)
Hindfoot (s.u.): *M* 17.0cm; *F* 16.2cm (16.0–16.3)
Ear (n.): *M* 8.0cm (7.4–8.5); *F* 7.9cm (7.0–8.9)
Adult weight: *F* 6.6kg (6.1–7.5)

From its first encounter with Europeans, this beautiful rock-wallaby whetted the apetites of fur traders, and this unfortunate attraction quickly brought the species under heavy pressure. Frederick Wood Jones, in a pessimistic mood in 1924, predicted that " . . . it will almost certainly disappear before very many years are past, since its pelt is far too attractive to permit it to survive as long as the fur trade exists."

Because Jones was specifically referring to the South Australian populations, it is ironic that it is now only in the Flinders Ranges of South Australia that the animal remains reasonably common. In western New South Wales and southwestern Queensland it is uncommon and possibly endangered.

The greatest dangers the species faces now are competition from introduced goats that have encroached into its rocky strongholds and predation from the fox.

Foods eaten vary seasonally but include forbs (e.g. *Cyanoglossum*) grasses (e.g. *Themida*) and browse (e.g. *Acacia* and *Callitris*). In good seasons, forbs are the most common foods while in dry seasons, they eat more browse.

In captivity, births occur throughout the year. The gestation period is about 32 days. Young are independent of the pouch by 195 days. One captive lived for 12 years and two months.

REFERENCES

Gordon, G., McGreevy, D.G. and Lawrie, B.C., 1978. The Yellow-footed Rock Wallaby, *Petrogale xanthopus* Gray (Macropodidae) in Queensland. *Aust. Wildl. Res.* 5:295–97.

Copley, P.B., 1983. Studies on the Yellow-footed Rock-wallaby, *Petrogale xanthopus* Gray (Marsupialia:Macropodidae) I. Distribution in South Australia. *Aust. Wildl. Res.* 10:47–61.

Copley, P.B., and Robinson, A.C., 1983. Studies on the Yellow-footed Rock-Wallaby, *Petrogale xanthopus* Gray (Marsupialia:Macropodidae) II. Diet. *Aust. Wildl. Res.* 10:63–76.

Dawson, T.J. and Ellis, B.A., 1979. Comparison of the diets of Yellow-footed Rock-wallabies and sympatric herbivores in western New South Wales. *Aust. Wildl. Res.* 6:245–54.

SWAMP WALLABY

Wallabia bicolor

STATUS: SECURE

SIZE:

Nose-vent: *M* 75.6cm (72.3–84.7); *F* 69.7cm (66.5–75.0)
Tail-vent: *M* 76.1cm (69.0–86.2); *F* 69.2cm (64.0–72.8)
Hindfoot (s.u.): *M* 21.7cm (19.6–23.8); *F* 20.5cm (19.4–21.5)
Ear (n.): *M* 8.5cm (8.3–8.6); *F* 8.1cm (7.6–8.5)
Adult weight: *M* 17.0kg (12.3–20.5); *F* 13.0kg (10.3–15.4)

It is a delight to note that the beautiful and intriguing Swamp Wallaby is alive and well throughout most of its pre-European range. Only in South Australia is it possible that it has suffered local extinction. However, even here it is not certain that it ever in fact occurred in South Australia despite early reports (prior to 1924).

As one of the few browsing wallabies to survive the late Cainozoic bloom of grazing kangaroos, its diet has been of considerable interest. In the wild, it eats almost exclusively browse such as ferns, hemlock, eucalypt leaves, dogwood, sedges and rushes but normally not the grasses and clovers favoured by so many other large kangaroos.

Edwards and Ealey (1975) summarized its catholic diet in captivity which may give some measure of its opportunistic capacities: "... *every kind* of native and exotic vegetation presented to it, not to mention bread, cheese, pastry, roast lamb and muttonfat".

Its choice of habitat is almost equally broad. Although it prefers wet or dry sclerophyll forests, they also occur in rainforests, woodland, heathland and even (one report) in mangroves. In most of these habitats it shelters in long dense grasses that develop as an understory.

Births occur between May and August. Pouch life lasts for about 250 days and adult females can raise one young every eight months. Sexual maturity is reached in about 15 months.

REFERENCES

Calaby, J.H., 1966. Mammals of the Upper Richmond and Clarence Rivers, New South Wales. *Techn. Pap. Div. Wildl. Res. C.S.I.R.O.* No. 10:1–55.

Edwards, G.P., and Ealey, E.H.M., 1975. Aspects of the ecology of the Swamp Wallaby *Wallabia bicolor* (Marsupialia:Macropodidae). *Aust. Mammal.* 1:307–17.

Finlayson, H.H., 1931. On mammals from the Dawson Valley, Queensland. Part I. *Trans. R. Soc. S. Aust.* 55:67–89.

Floyd, R.B., 1980. Density of *Wallabia bicolor* (Desmarest) (Marsupialia:Macropodidae) in eucalypt plantations of different ages. *Aust. Wildl. Res.* 7:333–37.

Kirkpatrick, T.H., 1970. The Swamp Wallaby in Queensland. *Qd Ag. J.* 96:335–36.

THE PARMA WALLABY

Macropus parma

STATUS: SECURE

SIZE:

Nose-vent: *M* 49.8cm (44.7–51.7); *F* 48.6cm (45.5–52.7)
Tail-vent: *M* 50.2 cm (44.4–52.6); *F* 47.5 cm (40.5–50.9)
Hindfoot (s.u.): *M* 14.2 cm (13.7–14.7); *F* 13.5 cm (13.1–13.9)
Ear (n.): *M* 6.9 cm (6.8–7.0); *F* 6.7 cm (6.5–6.9)
Adult weight: *M* 4.9kg (4.3–5.4); *F* 4.0kg (3.2–4.8)

The Parma Wallaby has a curious history of rediscovery. Having supposedly vanished from the mainland by 1932, it was rediscovered in 1965 on Kawau Island, off Auckland, New Zealand. It had been transported from mainland Australia in the mid-1880s to amuse and feed the local Europeans. At the time it was recognised as the supposedly extinct Parma Wallaby in 1965, it was being shot in the thousands because it was regarded as a threat to the Kawau pine plantations. Hasty efforts to re-establish these prodigal wallabies in Australia became pointless when surviving Australian populations were discovered in 1967 near Gosford, New South Wales. Now other mainland populations have been found in several areas of eastern New South Wales and the species is presumed to be in no danger.

The preferred habitat appears to be sclerophyll forests with a thick scrubby understorey. However, some have been found in rainforest and dry sclerophyll forest. They spend the day in the forest and come out at night to feed in areas of disturbed forest. Foods include Kangaroo Grass (*Themeda australis*).

Young are mostly born between February and June. The gestation period is about 35 days. Pouch life lasts for about 212 days. Females become sexually mature as early as 12 months of age.

REFERENCES

Maynes, G.M., 1973. Reproduction in the Parma Wallaby, *Macropus parma* Waterhouse. *Aust. J. Zool.* 21:331–51.

Maynes, G.M., 1974. Occurrence and field recognition of *Macropus parma. Aust. Zool.* 18:72–87.

Maynes, G.M., 1976. Growth of the Parma Wallaby, *Macropus parma* Waterhouse. *Aust. J. Zool.* 24:271–36.

Maynes, G.M., 1977. Distribution and aspects of the biology of the Parma Wallaby, *Macropus parma*, in New South Wales. *Aust. J. Wildl. Res.* 4:109–25.

Tammar Wallaby

Macropus eugenii

STATUS: SECURE

SIZE:

Nose-vent: *M* 64.3cm (59.0–68.0); *F* 58.6cm (52.0–63.0)
Tail-vent: *M* 41.1cm (38.0–45.0); *F* 37.9cm (33.0–44.0)
Hindfoot (s.u.): *M* 13.6cm (13.2–14.0); *F* 11.8cm
Ear (n.): *M* 5.4cm (4.7–6.0); *F* 5.0
Adult weight: *M* 7.5kg (6.0–10.0); *F* 5.5kg (4.0–6.0)

Not only was the Tammar Wallaby the first Australian kangaroo to be described by a European, it was also possibly the first record of an Australian marsupial. The Dutch navigator Francisco Pelsaert, in charge of the ill-fated *Batavia*, spotted a Tammar Wallaby on Houtman's Abrolhos Islands off Western Australia. His ship was wrecked on the Abrolhos in 1629.

Interestingly, the stranded Pelsaert, with considerable idle time on his hands, made some of the first observations about kangaroo reproduction. He noted of the Tammar that its pouch young " . . . were only the size of a bean, though at the same time perfectly proportioned". He went on to suggest, albeit erroneously, that " . . . it seems certain that they grow there out of the nipples of the mammae, from which they draw their food".

Ironically, in 1830 this same species was observed by the London Surgeon Alexander Collie to give birth in the way we now know to be correct. He watched the tiny young emerge at the cloaca and crawl unaided to the pouch with " . . . progress which was about as expeditious as a snail".

Populations were later discovered on the mainland and on other offshore islands of Western Australia and South Australia. The largest island population was discovered on Kangaroo Island. John Gould noted in 1863 that this species was safe here because the " . . . almost impenetrable scrub of dwarf *Eucalypti*, which covers nearly the whole of Kangaroo Island, will always afford it a secure asylum, from which in all probability it will never be extirpated. The vegetation being too poor to render it worth the expense of clearing". In a way he was right; it still survives on Kangaroo Island. Unfortunately, not all island populations were as lucky and the species has now been exterminated from Flinders Island (South Australia) and St. Peters Island.

REFERENCES

Andrewartha, H.G. and Barker, S., 1969. Introduction to a study of the ecology of the Kangaroo Island Wallaby, *Protemnodon eugenii* (Desmarest) within Flinder's Chase, Kangaroo Island, South Australia. *Trans. Proc. Roy. Soc. S. Aust.* 93:127–32.

Barker, S., 1971. The Dama Wallaby *Protemnodon eugenii* in captivity. *Int. Zoo. Ybk.* 11:17–20.

Inns, R.W., 1982. Age determination in the Kangaroo Island Wallaby, *Macropus eugenii* (Desmarest). *Aust. Wildl. Res.* 9:213–20.

Jones, F.W., 1924. "The mammals of South Australia. Part II. Containing the bandicoots and the herbivorous marsupials". Govt. Printer:Adelaide.

TOOLACHE WALLABY

Macropus greyi

STATUS: EXTINCT

SIZE:

Nose-vent: M 81.0cm; F 74.4cm (64.8–84.0)
Tail-vent: M 73.0cm; F 71.0cm
Hindfoot (s.u.): M 21.2cm; F 21.6cm
Ear (n.): M 6.5cm; F 7.1cm
Adult weight: F 6.0kg

Frederick Wood Jones remarked in 1924 that the once very common Toolache Wallaby was the "most beautiful and elegant of all of the wallabies". Unfortunately, this beauty is no longer in the eye of any beholder; Europeans exterminated the entire species. Jones noted at the time of his remark that only five or six individuals remained. This tragic situation came about because Europeans found this delightful target fun to shoot and profitable to sell as skins.

Two abortive last-minute efforts to save the remnants of the species took place, in 1923 and 1924. The intent was to capture individuals and transport them to a sanctuary. Both efforts failed when all of the animals caught died from the stresses of the drive.

The preferred habitat was evidently open grasslands where it rested and grazed. Shelter was sought by day on raised "islands" covered by the She-oak (*Casuarina stricta*).

Predators, besides humans, included wedge-tailed eagles. These were seen to attack and carry off joeys. Knowing this, European children used to raid the nests of the eagles to recover the scalps of these wallabies for which they would receive the sixpence bounty paid at the time on all marsupial scalps.

REFERENCES

Finlayson, H.H., 1927. Observations on the South Australian members of the subgenus, "Wallabia". *Trans. Proc. Roy. Soc. S. Aust.* 51:363–77.

Horton, D.R. and Murray, P., 1980. The extinct Toolache Wallaby (*Macropus greyi*) from a spring mound in North Western Tasmania. *Rec. Queen Vict. Mus.* 71:1–12.

Robinson, A.C., 1983. The Toolache Wallaby, one of South Australia's extinct mammals. *S. Aust. Nat.* 57:50.

Robinson, A.C. and Young, M.C. 1983. "The Toolache Wallaby (*Macropus greyi* Waterhouse)". *Dept. Env. Plan S. Aust. Spec. Publ. 1983.* No.2:1–54.

WESTERN BRUSH WALLABY

Macropus irma

STATUS: SECURE

SIZE:

Nose-vent: *F* 83.7cm
Tail-vent: *F* 68.6cm
Hindfoot (s.u.): *F* 20.3cm
Ear (n.): 8.9cm
Adult weight: 8kg (7.0–9.0)

John Gould was so struck by the intense markings of this wallaby that he was moved to remark in 1863 " . . . if its fore feet and the tips of its ears had been carefully dipped in ink, they could not be of a blacker hue, nor could this colouring terminate more abruptly. That there is no special end or purpose for the fantastic markings of the kangaroos and many other animals, beyond mere ornament, I think there cannot be a doubt".

Many contempory zoologists would take issue with Gould's last conclusion and suggest that the distinctive colours were probably the result of natural selection having led to gradual changes that favoured the species' ability to survive. For example, this wallaby's pattern might help it to remain camouflaged in bush that was frequently burnt. Perhaps it is more difficult for a predator to distinguish the outline of a motionless wallaby if its ears and hands resemble the burned ends of branches and bark that surround it.

Unfortunately, very little is known about this wallaby despite its abundance. It appears to favour open forests (e.g., it is abundant in Jarrah forest) and woodlands in which it feeds on grasses. Gould noted that in these habitats it was a very fast wallaby and difficult to catch. The breeding season is not well-known but young appear to be born in at least the months of April and May.

REFERENCES

Christensen, P., 1982. Western Brush Wallaby *Macropus irma*. P235 *in* "The Australian Museum complete book of Australian mammals" ed by R. Strahan. Angus and Robertson:Sydney.
Gould, J., 1863. "The mammals of Australia". The author:London.

WHIPTAIL WALLABY

Macropus parryi

STATUS: SECURE

SIZE:

Nose-vent: *M* 79.3cm (up to 92.4); *F* 73.2cm (64.8–75.5)
Tail-vent: *M* 94.1cm (86.1–104.5); *F* 78.1cm (72.8–85.8)
Hindfoot (s.u.): *M* 28.6cm; *F* 24.7cm
Ear (n.): *M* 10.5cm; *F* 9.8cm
Adult weight: *M* 16.0kg (14.0–26.0); *F* 11.0kg (7.0–15.0)

This wallaby seems designed for speed. John Gould noted in 1863: "So fleet is this animal, that it is only with the assistance of the finest dogs that there is any chance of procuring examples; it surpasses in fact every other animal in speed, and when fairly on the swing no dog can catch it".

The habitats of this wallaby include woodlands and most types of forests. They are most often seen on the open grassy floors of forests or in open country adjacent to forests. Here they eat grasses (e.g., kangaroo grass and even spear grass) or, more rarely, browse on shrubs or fern leaves.

Young have been noted in January. The gestation period is about 36 days. Average pouch life is 281 days. One captive individual lived for nine years and eight months.

This is one of the most sociable species of kangaroo. Although average group sizes are six, "mobs" (associations of groups) of 30 to 50 individuals have been noted. A social heirarchy develops among males, position in which is determined by fighting. The higher the rank, the greater the male's access to reproductive females.

REFERENCES

Calaby, J.H., 1966. Mammals of the Upper Richmond and Clarence Rivers, New South Wales. *Tech. Pap. Div. Wildl. Surv. C.S.I.R.O. Aust.* No. 10:1–55.

Finlayson, H.H., 1931, On mammals from the Dawson Valley, Queensland. Part I. *Trans. Proc. Roy. Soc. S. Aust.* 55:67–89.

Kaufman, J.H., 1974. Social ethology of the Whiptail Wallaby, *Macropus parryi* in northeastern New South Wales. *Anim. Behav.* 22:281–369.

Maynes, G.M., 1973. Aspects of reproduction in the Whiptail Wallaby, *Macropus parryi. Aust. Zool.* 18:43–46.

Steven, M., 1975. Observations on marsupials (Mammalia) at Ross River Dam, Townsville. *N. Qd Nat.* 42:6.

BLACK-STRIPED WALLABY

Macropus dorsalis

STATUS: SECURE

SIZE:

Nose-vent: *M* 152.5cm (142.0–159.0); *F* 115.0cm (112.0–121.0)
Tail-vent: *M* 76.5cm (74.0–83.0); *F* 59.5cm (54.0–61.5)
Hindfoot (s.u.): *M* 20.5cm; *F* 15.7cm
Ear (n.): *M* 8.8cm; *F* 8.3cm
Adult weight: *M* 18.0kg (16.0–20.0); *F* 6.5kg (6.0–7.5)

In 1931, Finlayson noted of this elegant wallaby that "Year in, year out, since the opening up of the country, it has been systematically snared and shot, but, in spite of the enormous destruction thus caused, its numbers are apparently little, if at all diminished. Residents of long standing have pointed out to me quite small patches of scrub which have been closely snared every winter for 40 years, and in which the species is as plentiful as ever". This situation has changed in so far as much of the original habitat suitable for this kangaroo has been destroyed. However, this species is now protected and still common in local areas.

This species prefers open sclerophyll forest but has been recorded from rainforest and brigalow scrub. In most of its habitats there is a dense canopy of tree and shrub species from 3 to 10 metres high.

The gestation period is about 30 to 35 days and pouch life lasts about 210 days. Females reach sexual maturity by about 14 months.

Evidently it is a very sociable rather than solitary wallaby because it has been observed that when groups of 20 or more individuals are disturbed while resting by day in camps, they move off in the same direction rather than scatter as individuals which is the more common reaction among kangaroos.

REFERENCES

Calaby, J.H., 1966. Mammals of the Upper Richmond and Clarence Rivers, New South Wales. *Techn. Pap. Div. Wildl. Res. C.S.I.R.O.* No. 10:1–55.

Finlayson, H.H., 1933. On mammals from the Dawson Valley, Queensland. Part I. *Trans. Proc. Roy. Soc. S. Aust.* 55:67–89.

Kirkpatrick, T.H., 1983. Black-striped Wallaby *Macropus dorsalis*. P238 *in* "The Australian Museum complete book of Australian mammals" ed by R. Strahan. Angus and Robertson:Sydney.

McCann, J., 1976. Distribution and habitat of *Wallabia dorsalis* in the Upper Clarence Region. *Bull. Aust. Mammal. Soc.* 3 (1):44.

RED-NECKED WALLABY

Macropus rufogriseus

STATUS: SECURE

SIZE:

Nose-vent: *M* 80.3cm (71.2–92.3); *F* 73.9cm (65.9–83.7)
Tail-vent: *M* 78.3cm (69.1–87.6); *F* 70.8cm (62.3–79.0)
Hindfoot (su): *M* 23.0cm; *F* 22.0cm
Ear (n): *M* 7.8cm, *F* 7.6cm
Adult weight: *M* 19.2kg (15.0–26.9); *F* 13.9kg (11.0–15.5)

This is a very secure wallaby. It is common in local areas of coastal woodland and sclerophyll forest from Rockhampton, Queensland to southeastern South Australia. It is now possibly even more abundant in Tasmania than it was before European settlement. This unusual situation is despite the fact that regular culling takes place, possibly because this species is advantaged by the steady clearing of dense forests taking place on that island.

The Tasmanian and mainland forms differ somewhat in their reproductive biology. While the mainland form produces young in all months, the Tasmanian form (Bennett's Wallaby) gives birth only between late January and early August. In both forms, the gestation period is about 30 days. Pouch life lasts for about 280 days and females become sexually mature by about 14 months. One individual was known to live for 17 years.

This species is mainly a browser although commonly it grazes on the grassed slopes adjoining the forests. Foods eaten include young shoots and leaves of heath plants such as those of grass trees (e.g. *Xanthorrhea semiplana*).

REFERENCES

Finlayson, H.H., 1930. Observations of the South Australian members of the subgenus, "Wallabia". *Trans. Proc. Roy. Soc. S. Aust.* 54:47–56.

McEvoy, J.S., 1970. The Red-necked Wallaby in Queensland. *Qd Ag. J.* 96:114–16.

Merchant, J.C. and Calaby, J.H., 1981. Reproductive biology of the Red-necked Wallaby *Macropus rufogriseus banksianus*) and Bennett's Wallaby (*M. r. rufogriseus*) in captivity. *J. Zool. London* 194:203–17.

WESTERN GREY KANGAROO

Macropus fuliginosus

STATUS: SECURE

SIZE:

Nose-vent: *M* 94.6–222.5cm; *F* 97.1–174.6cm
Tail-vent: *M* 42.5–100.0cm; *F* 44.3–81.5cm
Hindfoot (s.u.): *M* 32.5cm (32.0–33.0)
Ear (n.): *M* 12.0cm
Weight: *M* 3.0–53.5kg; *F* 4.5–27.5kg

The first specimen of this species to be named was collected from Kangaroo Island, South Australia in 1802. Frederick Wood Jones unflatteringly described this island kangaroo in 1924 as ". . . a lumbering, rather stupid looking creature, clumsily built, and . . . by far the slowest of all the kangaroos". The island was named in 1802 by Matthew Flinders in honour of this nevertheless very edible species.

Curiously, until Jones pointed out that not only were they still on that island but were regularly being converted in Adelaide into handbags and coats, most zoologists followed Gould in the belief that the species had never even occurred on the island.

Today it is clear that it is the same species as the common Grey Kangaroo of Western Australia and that it occurs in all of the eastern states except Tasmania. Clarification of its distinction from the Eastern Grey Kangaroo, however, had to await the serological studies of John Kirsch and Bill Poole.

The habitat requirements of the species are broad and it ranges from sclerophyll forest to semi-arid savannah and woodlands.

Births occur throughout the year but are more frequent in the summer months. The gestation period is about 30 days. At birth, young weigh just over 0.8gm. Pouch life lasts for about 320 days. Females begin to reproduce when they are about 17 months old.

REFERENCES

Kirsch, J.A.W. and Poole, W.E., 1972. Taxonomy and distribution of the grey kangaroos, *Macropus giganteus* Shaw and *Macropus fuliginosus* (Desmarest), and their subspecies (Marsupialia:Macropodidae). *Aust. J. Zool.* 20:315–39.

Poole, W.E., 1975. Reproduction in the two species of grey kangaroos, *Macropus giganteus* Shaw and *M. fuliginosus* (Desmarest) II. Gestation, parturition and pouch life. *Aust. J. Zool.* 23:333–53.

Poole, W.E. and Catling, P.C., 1974. Reproduction in the two species of grey kangaroos, *Macropus giganteus* Shaw and *M. fuliginosus* (Desmarest) I. Sexual maturity and oestrus. *Aust. J. Zool.* 22:277–302.

Schepherd, N.C., 1982. Extension of the known range of Western Grey Kangaroos, *Macropus fuliginosus*, and Eastern Grey Kangaroos, *M. giganteus*, in New South Wales. *Aust. Wildl. Res.* 9:389–91.

EASTERN GREY KANGAROO

Macropus giganteus

STATUS: SECURE

SIZE:

Nose-vent: *M* 97.2–230.2cm; *F* 95.8–185.7cm
Tail-vent: *M* 43.0–109.0cm; *F* 44.6–84.2cm
Hindfoot (s.u.): *M* 35.0cm (26.0–38.0) *F* 29.0cm (27.0–31.0)
Ear (n.): *M* 13.8
Weight: *M* 4.0–66.0kg; *F* 3.5–32.0kg

It has sometimes been said that the first thing Captain Cook's team did when they saw a kangaroo was to set the dog on it. Whether or not that's true, it appears to be the case that among the three kangaroos they collected in 1770, from what is now Cooktown in northeastern Queensland, were two Eastern Grey Kangaroos. The other was apparently a Common Wallaroo. After eating the kangaroos, Joseph Banks (with indigestion) added insult to injury by noting that it was ". . . certainly the most insipid meat . . ." he had ever eaten.

Habitats include sclerophyll forest, savannah woodlands, mallee, heath and cleared pasture, commonly in areas where annual rainfall exceeds 38cm. In semi-arid areas, such as western New South Wales, they occur along heavily wooded creeks.

Foods include perennial grasses (e.g., *Themida*) and some dicotyledons (e.g. *Indigoflora*). In dry areas, the diet may consist of 31 per cent spinifex (*Triodia*). Their food intake is only about half as much per kg of body weight as that of a sheep.

Births can occur throughout the year but are more common in March to May. Intervals between births average about 362 days. At birth they weigh about 0.9gm. The eyes open by about 200 days. Pouch life lasts about 284 days. Females mature sexually at about 17 months. Most individuals live less than 15 years but some have reached 18 years.

REFERENCES

Grant, T.R., 1973. Dominance and association among members of a captive and free-ranging group of Grey Kangaroos (*Macropus giganteus*). *Anim. Behav.* 21:449–56.

Hill, G.J.E., 1981. A study of habitat preferences in the Grey Kangaroo. *Aust. Wildl. Res.* 8:245–54.

Poole, W.E. 1983. Breeding in the Grey Kangaroo, *Macropus giganteus*, from widespread locations in eastern Australia. *Aust. Wildl. Res.* 10:453–66.

Russell, E.M., 1974. The biology of kangaroos (Marsupialia:Macropodidae). *Mamm. Rev.* 4:1–59.

Taylor, R.J., 1980. Distribution of feeding activity of the Eastern Grey kangaroo, *Macropus giganteus*, in coastal lowland of south-east Queensland. *Aust. Wildl. Res.* 7:317–25.

COMMON WALLAROO

Macropus robustus

STATUS: SECURE

SIZE:

Nose-vent: *M* 113.8–198.6cm; *F* 110.7–158.0cm
Tail-vent: *M* 55.1–90.1cm; *F* 53.4–74.9cm
Hindfoot (s.u.): *M* 29.8cm (29.5–30.0); *F* 24.2cm (22.0–25.7)
Ear (n.): *M* 12.5cm; *F* 11.9cm (11.6–12.1)
Weight: *M* 7.3–46.5kg; *F* 6.3–25.0kg

The distribution of this species as it appears on the map is misleading. Although technically widespread, because they are normally restricted to mountains, hills, ridges, rocky plateaus and sometimes tablelands, the actual distribution is very spotty. Nevertheless, they are very abundant in local areas and as a species this wallaroo is in no danger. It occurs in most habitats from arid grasslands to coastal rainforests.

In arid areas, they are normally tied to their rocky homes because of the need for caves or rock shelters in which to hide during the heat of the day. Now that Europeans have created many new watering points and this Wallaroo's need for shelter has become accordingly reduced, some populations have become established on the plains.

The diet depends to a large extent on the vegetation surrounding the shelter site. In arid areas, spinifex may make up 70 percent of the diet. Other grasses, shrubs, chenopods and herbs are also eaten.

Breeding can take place throughout the year but, if the season deteriorates, females will stop breeding until conditions improve. The gestation period is about 32 days. Pouch life lasts for about 256 days. Females mature sexually between 17 and 24 months of age. One captive individual lived for 18 years and seven months.

Geographic variation in aspects of the appearance and biology of this species is very marked. Prior to recent systematic molecular and chromosomal studies, this species was thought to represent three different kinds of wallaroo.

REFERENCES

Croft, D.B., 1981. Social behaviour of the Euro, *Macropus robustus* (Gould), in the Australian arid zone. *Aust. Wildl. Res.* 8:13–49.

Dawson, T.J., 1973. Thermoregulatory responses of the arid zone kangaroos, *Megaleia rufa* and *Macropus robustus. Comp. Biochem. Physiol.* 46A:153–69.

Ealey, E.H.M., 1967. Ecology of the Euro, *Macropus robustus* (Gould) in northwestern Australia. *C.S.I.R.O. Wildl. Res.* 12:9–80.

Russell, E.M. and Richardson, B.J., 1971. Some observations on the breeding, age structure, dispersion and habitat of populations of *Macropus robustus* and *Macropus antilopinus* (Marsupialia). *J. Zool. Lond.* 165:131–42.

Taylor, R.J., 1983. The diet of the Eastern Grey Kangaroo and Wallaroo in areas of improved and native pasture in the New England Tablelands. *Aust. Wildl. Res.* 10:203–11.

BLACK WALLAROO

Macropus bernardus

STATUS: VULNERABLE

SIZE:

Nose-vent: *M* 68.3cm (59.5–72.5); *F* 64.6cm
Tail-vent: *M* 60.9cm (54.5–64.0); *F* 57.5cm
Ear (n.): *M* 6.3cm (6.0–6.5)
Adult Weight: *M* 21.0kg (19.0–22.0); *F* 13.0kg

The taxonomic history of this splendid wallaroo is unusual. It was first described by Lord Rothschild as *Dendrodorcopsis woodwardi* probably because he was struck by what appeared to be a resemblance in build to the tree-kangaroos (genus *Dendrolagus*) and in colour to the forest wallabies of New Guinea (genus *Dorcopsis*). He was also honouring the Curator of the Perth Museum, Mr Bernard Woodward. A year later, having reconsidered the relationships of the animal, Rothschild decided that in fact it was a species of *Macropus*. But because Oldfield Thomas had already (in 1901) named a species *Macropus woodwardi* (which is now regarded to be a form of the Common Wallaroo), he had to give his new chocolate-coloured kangaroo a different name in order to avoid confusion. So, he renamed it *Macropus bernardus*.

Very little is known about the biology of this species; much less than for any of the other large kangaroos. It lives (commonly in pairs) only in the rugged boulder-strewn hillsides of Arnhem Land plateaus. These areas support a woodland with an understorey of grasses, herbs and shrubs of which it eats the first two. It spends the day in caves or among boulders and feeds on the slopes at night.

Adults with pouch-young have been collected in September and October.

REFERENCES

Parker, S.A., 1971. Notes on the small Black Wallaroo *Macropus bernardus* (Rothschild, 1904) of Arnhem land. *Vict. Nat.* 88:41–43.

Richardson, B.J. and Sharman, G.B., 1976. Biochemical and morphological observations on the wallaroos (Macropodidae:Marsupialia) with a suggested new taxonomy. *J. Zool. Lond.* 179:499–513.

Thomas, O., 1904. On a collection of mammals made by Mr J.T. Tunney in Arnhem Land, Northern Territory of South Australia. *Novit. Zool.* 11:222–29.

ANTILOPINE WALLAROO

Macropus antilopinus

STATUS: SECURE

SIZE:

Nose-vent: *M* 106.0cm (96.5–120.0); *F* 80.5cm (77.8–83.5)
Tail-vent: *M* 81.5cm (78.0–89.0); *F* 69.2cm (67.9–70.0)
Hindfoot (s.u.): *M* 32.6cm (31.2–34.0); *F* 26.7cm
Ear (n.): *M* 11.1cm (11.0-11.2); *F* 8.9cm
Adult weight: *M* 37.0kg (30.0–49.0); *F* 17.5kg (16.0–20.0)

John Gould provided a gloomy forecast in 1863 when he suggested that this species would ". . . soon be extirpated when Northern Australia becomes peopled by miners and stockholders". Fortunately for the Antilopine Wallaroo, this has not happened despite the firm establishment of the industries he foretold. In fact, in some areas of northern Australia, it is among the most common of the large kangaroos.

This grazing wallaroo is found in open forests and in relatively open savannah woodlands. In some regions they are seen near rocky escarpments but do not hesitate to move well out on to the flat plains. In other regions such as in Arnhem Land they are only rarely seen near escarpments.

This species is highly gregarious and commonly occurs in groups of 4 to 5 individuals. Large adult males and females with young-at-foot are, however, commonly excluded from these groups. Adults tend to groom each other which is not a common behaviour among kangaroos. This mutual grooming may be used to develop social bonds between individuals. Young are most commonly born in March and April.

REFERENCES

Calaby, J.H. and Keith, K., 1974. Mammals. Pp179–208 *in* "Fauna survey of the Port Essington District, Coburg Peninsula, Northern Territory of Australia" ed. by H.J. Frith and J.H. Calaby. *Techn. Pap. Div. Wildl. Surv. C.S.I.R.O. Aust.* No. 28.

Croft, D.B., 1982. Some observations on the behaviour of the Antilopine Wallaroo *Macropus antilopinus* (Marsupialia: Macropodidae). *Aust. Mammal.* 5:5–13.

Dahl, K., 1897. Biological notes on North-Australian Mammalia. *The Zoologist (4)* 1:189–216.

Russell, E.M. and Richardson, B.J., 1971. Some observations on the breeding, age structure, dispersion and habitat of populations of *Macropus robustus* and *Macropus antilopinus* (Marsupialia). *J. Zool. Lond.* 165:131–42.

RED KANGAROO

Macropus rufus

STATUS: SECURE

SIZE:

Nose-vent: *M* 115.0cm (93.5–140.0); *F* 100.0cm (74.5–110.0)
Tail-vent: *M* 88.0cm (71.0–100.0); *F* 82.0cm (64.5–90.0)
Hindfoot (s.u.): *M* 36cm; *F* 29.2cm (25.8–31.8)
Ear (n.): *M* 11.0cm; *F* 12.4cm (11.0–13.7)
Adult weight: *M* 66.0kg (22.0–85.0); *F* 26.5kg (17.0–35.0)

In discussing this "most beautiful member of the family", John Gould warned in 1863: "I regret very much to say that the time may not be far distant when an opportunity of giving a full-sized drawing of the head of this noble animal, taken from life, will not be possible. The larger and more conspicuous productions of an island are often, as a natural consequence, the first that become extirpated". The plight of the Tasmanian Thylacine and the Kangaroo Island Emu serve to show that often the general proposition is correct. But, in this case, it is a pleasure to note that he was wrong – the Red Kangaroo is alive and doing very well indeed.

Although at the time of European settlement it occurred east of the Dividing Range, since Europeans arrived and the extensive development of artificial watering points, this species has almost certainly increased its range and numbers in the more arid areas.

The modern range of this large grazing kangaroo depends as much on the distribution of green grass as it does on water. They seem to prefer the open plains and savannahs of inland Australia but occasionally occupy woodlands and even dry sclerophyll forest.

The reproductive cycle of this species is well-known. Breeding may occur throughout the year but is more common in the spring and summer. The gestation period is about 33 days, the eyes open at about 130 days, the young leaves the pouch by about 240 days and females mature sexually by about two to three years. The oldest captive individual lived for 16 years and four months.

As well as humans, dingoes are significant predators. In one study carried out over seven weeks, a group of five dingoes killed 83 Red Kangaroos within 150 metres of a watering point.

REFERENCES

Croft, D.B., 1981. Behaviour of Red Kangaroos, *Macropus rufus* (Desmarest, 1822) in northwestern New South Wales, Australia. *Aust. Mammal.* 4:5–58.

Johnson, C.N., 1983. Variations in group size and composition in Red and Western Grey Kangaroos, *Macropus rufus* (Desmarest) and *M. fuliginosus* (Desmarest). *Aust. Wildl. Res.* 10:25–31.

Low, W.A., Muller, W.J., Dudzinski, M.L. and Low, B.S., 1981. Population fluctuations and range community preference of Red Kangaroos in central Australia. *J. Applied Ecol.* 18:27–36.

Russell, E.M., 1974. The biology of kangaroos (Marsupialia: Macropodidae). *Mammal. Rev.* 4:1–59.

Sharman, G.B. and Calaby, J.H., 1964. Reproductive behaviour in the Red Kangaroo, *Megaleia rufa,* in captivity. *C.S.I.R.O. Wildl. Res.* 9:58–85.

Shepherd, N.C., 1981. Predation of Red Kangaroos, *Macropus rufus,* by the Dingo, *Canis familiaris dingo* (Blumenbach), in northwestern New South Wales. *Aust. Wildl. Res.* 8:255–62.

Species of Australia and New Guinea

THE AGILE WALLABY.

RED-LEGGED PADEMELON

Thylogale stigmatica

STATUS: SECURE

SIZE:

Nose-vent: *M* 49.2cm (47.0–53.6); *F* 46.3cm (38.6–52.0)
Tail-vent: *M* 44.3cm (37.2–47.3); *F* 35.7cm (30.1–44.5)
Hindfoot (s.u.): *M* 13.4cm (13.3–13.4); *F* 12.4cm (12.0–13.3)
Ear (n.): *M* 6.4cm; *F* 6.4cm (6.3–6.5)
Adult weight: *M* 5.1kg (3.7–6.8); *F* 4.2kg (2.5–4.1)

Mr Macgillivray noted in the "Voyage of the *HMS Rattlesnake*" that while they were tacking in-shore ". . . a native dog was seen by Lieut. Simpson in chase of a small kangaroo, which, on being close pressed, plunged into the water and swam out to sea, when it was picked up by the boat, leaving its pursuer standing on a rock, gazing wistfully at its intended prey, until a musket-ball, which went very near its mark, sent it off at a trot". This small kangaroo turned out to be a species then new to science, the Red-legged Pademelon.

This pademelon is one of only two species of kangaroo that occur in New Guinea as well as Australia. Its overall status in New Guinea is uncertain.

In Australia it is not particularly common anywhere but is widespread and, for this reason, probably secure.

Preferred habitat for this species, as for all pademelons, is rainforest but they also occur in other forest habitats particularly if these are adjacent to rainforest.

Foods known to be eaten include mostly browse but also some grasses. Grasses are gathered from fields adjacent to the forest or from clearings caused by fallen trees.

Unlike the Red-necked Pademelon, this species spends most of its time within the rainforest and, as a result, in areas where the two species overlap, the Red-legged Pademelon is the less frequently seen of the two.

REFERENCES

Brass, L.J., 1953. Results of the Archbold Expeditions. No. 68. Summary of the 1948 Cape York (Australia) Expedition. *Bull. Amer. Mus. Nat. Hist.* 102:139–205.

Breeden, S. and Breeden, K., 1970. "Tropical Queensland. A natural history of Australia. 1". Collins:Sydney.

Calaby, J.H., 1966. Mammals of the Upper Richmond and Clarence Rivers, New South Wales. *Techn. Pap. Div. Wildl. Surv. C.S.I.R.O. Aust.* No. 10:1–55.

Troughton, E. LeG., 1951. The kangaroo family. The pademelons or scrub-wallabies – I. *Aust. Mus. Mag.* 10:218–22.

Winter, J.W., 1973. Rainforest mammals. *Wildl. Aust.* 10:84–86.

AGILE WALLABY

Macropus agilis

STATUS: SECURE

SIZE:

Nose-vent: *M* 80.0cm (67.5–85.0); *F* 65.0cm (59.3–72.2
Tail-vent: *M* 77.0cm (69.2–84.0); *F* 64.0cm (58.7–70.0)
Hindfoot (s.u.): *M* 23.3cm (21.5–24.5); *F* 21.8cm (20.7–23.0)
Ear (n.): *M* 8.3cm (7.8–8.8); *F* 7.9cm (7.5–8.2)
Adult weight: *M* 19.0kg (16.0–27.0); *F* 11.0kg (9.0–15.0)

This is one of the largest of the wallabies and one of the most secure. Its modern-day range across northern and down northeastern Australia is essentially unchanged from the time of European settlement. Even the outlying population on Stradbroke Island in southeastern Queensland seems secure.

Charles Hoy noted in 1920 that in areas of the Northern Territory, on the plains along river banks, mobs of over 200 individuals were sometimes seen feeding together. Normally, however, they rarely associate in groups of more than a few individuals.

Their preferred habitat seems to include the grassed borderlands and pandanus fringes of river banks and billabongs as well as the tropical woodlands along the river floodplains. Some have been known to frequent sandy beaches and even mangrove swamps.

They have been observed when thirsty to dig soakage holes in the sandbanks adjoining the rivers, rather than risk drinking from the crocodile-infested rivers themselves.

They are opportunistic feeders and are known to consume green grass, dry spear grass and browse such as *Melaleuca* saplings and low shrubs.

Young are born throughout the year with females able to give birth every seven months. The gestation period is 29.2 days and pouch life lasts about 219 days.

REFERENCES

Bell, H.M., 1973. The ecology of three macropod marsupial species in an area of open forest and savannah woodland in north Queensland, Australia. *Mammalia* 37:527–44.

Husson, A.M., 1958. Notes on *Protemnodon agilis papuanus* (Peters and Doria) from New Guinea (Mammalia: Marsupialia). *Nova Guinea* 9:245–52.

Johnson, P.M., 1980. Field observations on group compositions in the Agile Wallaby, *Macropus agilis* (Gould) (Marsupialia: Macropodidae). *Aust. Wildl. Res.* 7:327–31.

Kirkpatrick, T.H., 1970. The Agile Wallaby in Queensland. *Qd Ag. J.* 96:179–80.

Merchant, J.C., 1976. Breeding biology of the Agile Wallaby, *Macropus agilis* (Gould) (Marsupialia: Macropodidae), in captivity. *Aust. Wildl. Res.* 3:93–103.

SPECIES OF NEW GUINEA

BLACK DORCOPSIS

Dorcopsis atrata

STATUS: VULNERABLE

SIZE:

Nose-vent: *M* 86.0cm (73.3–99.5); *F* 82.3cm
Tail-vent: *M* 33.6cm (28.5–38.2); *F* 32.9cm
Hindfoot (s.u.): *M* 10.9cm (10.0–11.7); *F* 10.2cm
Ear (n.): *M* 3.7cm (3.5–3.8); *F* 3.3cm
Adult weight: *M* 4.8kg (2.8–6.6); *F* 3.9kg

The Black Dorcopsis is restricted to high mountain forests on Goodenough and possibly nearby Fergusson Islands off the northeastern coast of New Guinea. Until 1953 this little wallaby remained unknown to Europeans, hidden away in its mountain stronghold. Hobart Van Deusen, describer of the species, said of its forest home ". . . when the clouds blanket this jagged upland it is a dark world of swirling mists and dripping leaves. The pervading quiet is broken only by the occasional screech of a parrot or thrumming wings of a hornbill. This is the world of the Black Dorcopsis. . . "

The Black Dorcopsis is distinctive in living in such mountainous areas. All of its mainland relatives are found only in lowland forests, never above 400 metres. Because of its cold habitat, the coat of the Black Dorcopsis is dense and luxurious. While the outer hairs are black, the dense underfur is white, giving the species an attractive appearance.

Nothing is known of the life history of the Black Dorcopsis. However, because it is so different in ecology and appearance from its mainland relatives, zoologists surmise that it must have reached its island home long ago.

REFERENCES

George, G., 1973. Land mammal fauna. *Aust. Nat. Hist.* 17:420–26.
Van Deusen, H.M., 1957. Results of the Archbold Expeditions. No. 76. A new species of wallaby (genus *Dorcopsis*) from Goodenough Island, Papua. *Amer. Mus. Novit.* 1826.

BROWN DORCOPSIS

Dorcopsis veterum

STATUS: SECURE

SIZE

Nose-vent: *M* 82.5cm; *F* 53.0cm
Tail-vent: *M* 50.0cm; *F* 38.0cm
Hindfoot (s.u.): *M* 15.6cm; *F* 11.3cm
Ear (n.): *M* 4.2cm; *F* 3.5cm

The mighty Fly River forms a barrier that separates the Brown and Grey Dorcopsis Wallabies of southern New Guinea. The Brown Dorcopsis inhabits lowland rainforest below 400 metres to the west of the Fly, extending as far west as the Vogelkop Peninsula in the far west of the island.

The skin can easily be seen under the thin fur of the Brown Dorcopsis and the thin covering of fine fur in this species is doubtless all that is required to insulate the animal in its hot, humid environment. *Dorcopsis* means gazelle-faced and it is often easier to see the resemblance to a gazelle in the face of the dorcopsis wallabies than it is to discern their kangaroo pedigree. Indeed, their long, dropping muzzle makes them look most un-kangaroo like. In part because the Brown Dorcopsis is found in areas rarely frequented by Europeans, we know almost nothing of its habits or ecology.

REFERENCES

George, G., 1973. Land mammal fauna. *Aust. Nat. Hist.* 17:420–26.

Zeigler, A.C., 1983. An ecological check-list of New Guinea Recent mammals. Pp862–92 *in* "Biogeography and ecology in New Guinea" ed by J.L. Gressitt. Junk:the Hague.

GREY DORCOPSIS

Dorcopsis luctuosa

STATUS: SECURE

SIZE

Nose-vent: *M* 71.2cm; *F* 52.5cm
Tail-vent: *M* 41.9cm; (38.8–45.0); *F* 31.0cm
Hindfoot (s.u.) *M* 12.5cm (11.9–13.1); *F* 11.1cm
Ear (n.): *M* 6.2cm (6.0–6.3); *F* 5.3cm
Adult weight: *M* 11.6kg; *F* 3.6kg

The Grey Dorcopsis and indeed all dorcopsis wallabies have long faces, short feet and unusual, short tails which are held off the ground when the animals are resting. Only the tip of the tail contacts the ground. The tail tip lacks hairs and is heavily cornified. The reasons for this unusual habit and morphology are unknown, but some zoologists suggest this adaptation may keep the tail beyond the reach of hungry leeches.

Tourists who visit Koki market in Port Moresby are probably familiar with the Grey Dorcopsis, although they may not be aware of it. Each day a large number of smoked carcasses of this species is offered for sale, not only at Koki, but in many markets throughout southeastern Papua. Judging by the numbers caught, the Grey Dorcopsis must be abundant, even in the vicinity of large towns such as Port Moresby. Near Port Moresby, the Grey Dorcopsis probably inhabits the small remaining patches of rainforest such as those along water courses or in protected valleys. Despite its abundance close to the national capital, the habits and ecology of the Grey Dorcopsis still remain unstudied.

REFERENCES

George, G., 1973. Land mammal fauna. *Aust. Nat. Hist.* 17:420–26.

Zeigler, A.C., 1983. An ecological check-list of New Guinea Recent mammals. Pp862–92 *in* "Biogeography and ecology in New Guinea" ed by J.L. Gressitt. Junk:the Hague.

WHITE-STRIPED DORCOPSIS

Dorcopsis hageni

STATUS: SECURE

SIZE

Nose-vent: *M* 62.0cm; *F* 58.7cm (54.4–63.0)
Tail-vent: *M* 42.8cm; *F* 38.8cm (38.2–39.5)
Hindfoot (s.u.): *M* 14.2cm; *F* 12.6cm (12.5–12.7)
Ear (n.): *M* 5.3cm; *F* 4.7cm (4.2–5.1)

The White-striped Dorcopsis is the largest of the New Guinea dorcopsis wallabies. It is an animal of the steamy, luxurious lowland rainforests of northern New Guinea, a country where vast rivers such as the Sepik and Idenburg wind their way lazily over hundreds of miles of swampy, flat land towards the sea.

Although the White-striped Dorcopsis is thinly-furred, its attractive coat is very sleek and fine. Its fawnish-brown basal colour and distinct white stripe running down the centre of the back makes a most attractive colour pattern.

As with all of the New Guinea forest wallabies, the male of the White-striped Dorcopsis is considerably larger than the female. Because of the dense jungle that is its home, the White-striped Dorcopsis is usually seen only on river banks. Daylight sightings in these areas suggest it may be partly diurnal. While it is quite common in parts of its range, any plans to extensively log its vulnerable lowland rainforest home could be disastrous for the species.

REFERENCES

George, G., 1973. Land mammal fauna. *Aust. Nat. Hist.* 17:420–26.
Zeigler, A.C., 1983. An ecological check-list of New Guinea Recent mammals. Pp862–92 *in* "Biogeography and ecology in New Guinea" ed by J.L. Gressitt. Junk:the Hague.

LITTLE DORCOPSIS

Dorcopsulus vanheurni

STATUS: SECURE

SIZE

Nose-vent: *M* 39.0cm; *F* 38.0cm
Tail-vent: *M* 31.0cm; *F* 23.8cm (22.5–25.0)
Hindfoot (s.u.) *M* 9.5cm; *F* 9.2cm (9.0–9.4)
Ear (n.): *M* 4.0cm; *F* 3.6cm (3.5–3.6)

The Little Dorcopsis is the smallest of the kangaroos of New Guinea, being about the size of a hare. It inhabits mossy montane forests along the entire length of the central New Guinean Cordillera except the Vogelkop Peninsula. This tiny animal is very fast and agile. Hunters often have difficulty securing it because it is too fast for most dogs. Its long, dense, chocolate-brown coat protects it from the cold and damp of its forest home and also camoflages it in its sombre environment.

Apart from the fact that is is nocturnal, the habits and life history of the Little Dorcopsis are largely unknown. However, when resting it lays a little more of its tail on the ground than do the larger dorcopsis wallabies but not as much as typical kangaroos and wallabies. The Little Dorcopsis probably eats leaves and possibly some fallen fruit.

REFERENCES

George, G., 1973. Land mammal fauna. *Aust. Nat. Hist.* *17*:420–26.
Zeigler, A.C., 1983. An ecological check-list of New Guinea Recent mammals. Pp862–92 *in* "Biogeography and ecology in New Guinea" ed by J.L. Gressitt. Junk:the Hague.

MACLEAY'S DORCOPSIS

Dorcopsulus macleayi

STATUS: VULNERABLE

SIZE

Nose-vent: 47.0cm
Tail-vent: 32.0cm
Hindfoot (s.u.) 10.5cm
Ear (n.): 3.0cm

Macleay's Dorcopsis is a rare animal, being known only from a handful of specimens that were collected on three or four occasions. It is restricted to a narrow altitudinal band of forest in the eastern part of New Guinea. The mid-montane forests that it inhabits are lower than those used by the Little Dorcopsis but above those used by the larger dorcopsis wallabies. These forests are dominated by huge *Araucaria* trees that stand high above the rainforest canopy. These forests giants are valuable for their timber and, if heavily exploited, the home of Macleay's Dorcopsis may be irreparably damaged.

A little larger than its near relative the Little Dorcopsis, Macleay's Dorcopsis is even less-known and more mysterious. However, in size, habitat and possibly relationships it appears to be between the Little Dorcopsis and the larger dorcopsis wallabies.

REFERENCES

George, G., 1979. The status of endangered Papua New Guinea mammals. Pp93–100 *in* "The status of endangered Australasian wildlife" ed by M. Tyler. Royal Zoological Society of South Australia:Adelaide.

Zeigler, A.C., 1983. An ecological check-list of New Guinea Recent mammals. Pp862–92 *in* "Biogeography and ecology in New Guinea" ed by J.L. Gressitt. Junk:the Hague.

GRIZZLED TREE-KANGAROO

Dendrolagus inustus

STATUS: VULNERABLE

SIZE

Nose-vent: *M* 72.3cm; *F* 62.5cm
Tail-vent: *M* 69.8cm; *F* 61.5cm
Hindfoot (s.u.): *M* 16.7cm; *F* 15.4cm
Ear (n.): *M* 6.1cm; *F* 5.7cm
Adult weight: *M* 11.0–14.5kg; *F* 10.0kg

The Grizzled Tree-kangaroo is the only New Guinean representative of a primitive group of tree-kangaroos that includes both Australian species. It is the least arboreally-adapted of the New Guinean tree-kangaroos and apparently is the least able climber.

The Grizzled Tree-kangaroo is found in hill forests from the Vogelkop area eastwards along the north coastal range to a point just east of the Irian Jaya-New Guinea border. It is a distinctive species with its "grizzled" appearance, relatively long feet and peculiar bald, cornified area on the top surface of the base of the tail. This latter feature may aid this species to sit in the crotch of a branch with its long tail tucked between its legs.

Partly because of its restricted distribution, the Grizzled Tree-kangaroo is one of the least-known and least-studied of New Guinean tree-kangaroos. Food preferences and other aspects of its ecology are unknown.

REFERENCES

Flannery, T.F. and Szalay, F., 1982. *Bohra paulae*, a new giant fossil tree kangaroo (Marsupialia: Macropodidae) from New South Wales, Australia. *Aust. Mammal.* 5:83–94.

Ganslosser, U., 1981. Vergleichende Untersuchungen zur Kletterfähigkeit einiger Baumkanguruharten (*Dendrolagus* Muller, 1839). *Zool Anz. Jena* 206:62–86.

GOODFELLOW'S TREE-KANGAROO

Dendrolagus goodfellowi

STATUS: VULNERABLE

SIZE

Nose-vent: *M* 58.0cm (57.4–58.5); *F* 58.8cm (56.0–63.5)
Tail-vent: *M* 70.4cm (69.0–71.8); *F* 69.1cm (58.5–75.7)
Hindfoot (s.u.): *M* 13.0cm (12.1–13.8); *F* 11.7cm (10.5–14.0)
Ear (n.): *M* 6.0cm (5.6–6.1); *F* 5.9cm (5.7–6.6)
Adult weight: *M* 7.5kg; *F* 7.4kg

Smallest and most attractive of the tree-kangaroos, Goodfellow's Tree-kangaroo is an inhabitant of the oak and lower beech forests of eastern New Guinea. Its main habitat, the oak forest, is so called because several species of rainforest-dwelling oaks are the dominant large trees of the forest at these altitudes. The acorns of some rainforest oaks are very large (up to 4cm in diameter) and it is surprising to find the rainforest floor in these areas littered with giant acorns.

The beautiful reddish-brown fur, double golden stripe down the back and the long mottled gold and reddish-brown tail of Goodfellow's Tree-kangaroo make it a particularly attractive and striking species. However, this pattern disguises the animal in its forest home and it is extremely difficult to locate one when it is resting by day in the rainforest canopy.

In the central highlands of New Guinea, Goodfellow's Tree-kangaroo has declined markedly since the coming of Europeans and in some areas has even become extinct. As human populations around New Guinea grow, it is possible that a similar pattern of demise may occur throughout its range.

REFERENCES

George, G., 1979. The status of endangered Papua New Guinea mammals. Pp93–100 *in* "The status of endangered Australasian wildlife" ed by M. Tyler. Royal Zoological Society of South Australia:Adelaide.

MATSCHIE'S TREE-KANGAROO

Dendrolagus matschiei

STATUS: VULNERABLE

SIZE

Nose-vent: *M* 63.8cm (61.5–66.0); *F* 60.8cm (58.3–62.5)
Tail-vent: *M* 58.8cm (55.5–62.0); *F* 61.8cm (55.7–68.5)
Hindfoot (s.u.): *M* 12.3cm (12.2–12.4); *F* 11.6cm (11.3–12.1)
Ear (n.): *M* 5.9cm (5.8–5.9); *F* 5.7cm (5.1–6.4)
Adult weight: *M* 10.4kg; *F* 10.4kg

Matschie's Tree-kangaroo is a near relative of Goodfellow's Tree-kangaroo, differing from it mainly in its more sombre colour pattern, its shorter tail, more robust build and larger size. Matschie's Tree-kangaroo is found only on the mountainous Huon Peninsula of northern New Guinea. The Huon Peninsula is separated from the central mountain range of New Guinea by deep river valleys, and as a result many of the animal species found there differ slightly from their relatives of the main range. Matschie's Tree-kangaroo probably developed from an ancestral population of Goodfellow's Tree-kangaroo isolated on the Huon Peninsula long ago. Because Doria's Tree-Kangaroo is not present on the Huon Peninsula, Matschie's Tree-kangaroo is found even in the high forests usually inhabited by the former species. This shift in ecology may account for many of the differences between the species of Matschie's and Goodfellow's Tree-kangaroos.

REFERENCES

Groves, C., 1982. The systematics of tree kangaroos (*Dendrolagus*:Marsupialia, Macropodidae). *Aust. Mammal.* 5:157–86.

DORIA'S TREE-KANGAROO

Dendrolagus dorianus

STATUS: VULNERABLE

SIZE

Nose-vent: *M* 69.6cm (67.0–73.0); *F* 62.7cm (59.6–67.5)
Tail-vent: *M* 55.9cm (52.0–58.5); *F* 56.3cm (46.6–66.2)
Hindfoot (s.u.): *M* 12.1cm (11.5–13.0); *F* 10.6cm (10.0–11.7)
Ear (n.): *M* 5.2cm (4.5–5.7); *F* 5.1cm (4.5–6.6)
Adult weight: *M* 15.0–18.0kg; *F* 8.0–13.0kg

Doria's Tree-kangaroo is the largest marsupial to inhabit the upland rainforests of New Guinea. Its eerie home is high in the moss forest where the trees are festooned with epiphytic ferns and orchids and great clumps of moss are nestled in the forks of branches, some as large as small cars. However, in southestern New Guinea it is also found at lower altitudes. For much of the day Doria's Tree-kangaroo remains hidden in the treetops, looking rather like another mass of brownish-green moss. However, in the evening it becomes active and begins to forage. Doria's Tree-kangaroo is unusual among tree-kangaroos in that it spends more time on the ground than other species (this is so at least in captivity where it has been closely observed).

Doria's Tree-kangaroo appears to be a more social species than other tree-kangaroos. Related females have been observed to gang together to protect each other from the aggressive actions of dominant males. Females will play with young other than their own.

For its size, Doria's Tree-kangaroo is an immensely powerful animal and hunters report that it can easily kill hunting dogs if they are unaided in the struggle by their owner. When not defending itself, however, Doria's Tree-kangaroo appears to be a gentle giant, eating mainly the leaves and possibly fruits of rainforest trees.

REFERENCES

Ganslosser, U., 1979. Soziale Interaktionen des Doria-baumkanguruhs (*Dendrolagus dorianus* Ramsay, 1883) (Marsupialia:Macropodidae). *Z. Saugthierd* 44:1–18.

Groves, C., 1982. The systematics of tree kangaroos (*Dendrolagus*: Marsupialia, Macropodidae). *Aust. Mammal.* 5:157–86.

Vogelkop Tree-kangaroo

Dendrolagus ursinus

STATUS: VULNERABLE

SIZE

Nose-vent: *M* 62.5cm
Tail-vent: *M* 42.3–47.8cm approx.
Hindfoot (s.u.): *M* 11.0–12.8cm approx.
Ear (n.): *M* 6.5cm

Few people realize that Indonesia has its own indigenous species of kangaroos. Of the two species restricted to Indonesia, the Vogelkop Tree-kangaroo is the better-known, the other species being the possibly extinct Christensen's Thylogale. As its name suggests, Indonesia's unique tree-kangaroo is restricted to the picturesquely-named Vogelkop (Bird's Head) Peninsula of far western Irian Jaya. The dark fur and shortened, bear-like face are alluded to in the species' scientific name *ursinus*, which is Latin for "bear-like".

An inhabitant of the treetops, the Vogelkop Tree-kangaroo is closely related to Doria's, Matschie's and Goodfellows's Tree-kangaroos. This group of species is restricted to New Guinea, and they are the group of tree-kangaroos that are best adapted morphologically for an arboreal existence.

The Vogelkop Tree-kangaroo is poorly known. However, in captivity it is reported to eat wild figs and young leaves and to live almost entirely on this diet for part of the year. The only noise it is known to make is a soft growl.

REFERENCES

Groves, C., 1982. The systematics of tree kangaroos (*Dendrolagus*: Marsupialia, Macropodidae). *Aust. Mammal.* 5:157–86.

Husson, A.M. and Rappard, F.W., 1958. Note on the taxonomy and the habits of *Dendrolagus ursinus* Temminck and *D. leucogenys* Matschie (Mammalia:Marsupialia). *Nova Guinea (ns)* 9:9–14.

DUSKY PADEMELON

Thylogale brunii

STATUS: SECURE

SIZE

Nose-vent: *M* 54.5cm
Tail-vent: *M* 42.5cm; *F* 39.3cm (39.0–39.5)
Hindfoot (s.u.): *M* 13.5cm; *F* 13.9cm (12.8–14.9)
Ear (n.): *M* 5.3cm; *F* 5.2cm (4.9–5.4)

Seen by a European naturalist as early as 1711 in a menagerie in Java, the Dusky Pademelon was the first kangaroo to receive a scientific name. It is found only in New Guinea and some nearby islands. However, it has the widest distribution of any of the endemic kangaroos of New Guinea. It is the only kangaroo species found on New Britain and New Ireland to the north of New Guinea and the only species found on the Aru Islands to the south. The only areas of New Guinea not inhabited by this species are parts of the western third of the island.

The Dusky Pademelon is abundant in some areas where the high montane forest meets subalpine grasslands. Here it shelters in the dense forests during the day and emerges at night to feed on grasses and herbs in the subalpine grasslands.

Several races of Dusky Pademelon are currently recognised. However, future research may prove that some of these races are in fact distinct species, because they differ from each other in a number of ways. For instance, the race of Dusky Pademelon inhabiting the subalpine grasslands has denser fur, slightly different colouration and a slightly different skull than the race that occupies the lower hill forest.

REFERENCES

George, G., 1973. Land mammal fauna. *Aust. Nat. Hist.* 17:420–26.

Zeigler, A.C., 1983. An ecological check-list of New Guinea Recent mammals. Pp862–92 *in* "Biogeography and ecology in New Guinea" ed by J.L. Gressitt. Junk:the Hague.

THE MOUNTAINS OF IRIAN JAYA AND (BELOW) THE SKULL OF CHRISTENSEN'S PADEMELON.

CHRISTENSEN'S PADEMELON

Thylogale christenseni

STATUS: EXTINCT

SIZE

External measurements unknown

Perhaps the most mysterious animal in all of New Guinea, Christensen's Pademelon in known only from a handful of bones left over from the meal of a prehistoric New Guinean hunter. Its bones, about 5,000 years old, suggest that Christensen's Pademelon was a small animal about the size of the Little Dorcopsis. Its remains were found in a rockshelter high in the Carstenz Mountains of Irian Jaya. This area is so unexplored that zoologists cannot discount the possibility that this intriguing animal may still exist in the shadow of the mighty Carstenz Glacier. What makes the continued existence of this animal all the more plausible is the fact that the bones of all the animals found with those of Christensen's Pademelon represent species still living in New Guinea. One day, perhaps, the vast alpine grasslands of the Carstenz will reveal to an adventurous zoologist its best kept secret – a living Christensen's Pademelon.

REFERENCES

Hope, J.H., 1981. A new species of *Thylogale* (Marsupialia:Macropodidae) from Mapala rock shelter, Jaya (Carstenz) Mountains, Irian Jaya (Western New Guinea), Indonesia. *Rec. Aust. Mus.* 33:369–87.

GENERAL REFERENCES ABOUT KANGAROOS

There are 18 references that contain much information relevant to the whole of Australia and/or New Guinea.

Archer, M. and Clayton, G. (eds), 1984. "Vertebrate zoogeography and evolution in Australasia". Hesperian Press: Perth.

Collins, L.R., 1973. "Monotremes and marsupial: the other mammals". Edward Arnold: London.

Evans, D.D. (ed.), 1982. "The management of Australian mammals in captivity". Zoological Board of Victoria: Melbourne.

George, G., 1979. The status of endangered Papua New Guinea mammals. Pp 93–100 *in* Tyler (1979; see below)

Gould, J., 1863. "Mammals of Australia". The author: London.

Groves, R.H. and Ride, W.D.L. (eds), 1982. "Species at risk: research in Australia". Australian Academy of Science: Canberra.

Hume, I.D., 1982. "Digestive physiology and nutrition of marsupials". Cambridge University Press: Cambridge.

Nelson, J.E. (ed.), 1978. "A symposium on the phylogeny and evolution of Macropodidae". Volume 2 of *Australian Mammalogy*.

Ride, W.D.L., 1970. "A guide to the native mammals of Australia". Oxford University Press: Melbourne.

Russell, E.M., 1974. The biology of kangaroos (Marsupialia: Macropodidae). *Mammal. Rev.* 4:1–59.

Strahan, R. (ed.), 1983. "The Australian Museum complete book of Australian mammals". Angus and Robertson: Sydney.

Tate, G.H.H., 1948. Results of the Archbold Expeditions. No. 59. Studies on the anatomy and phylogeny of the Macropodidae (Marsupialia). *Bull. Amer. Mus. Nat. Hist.* 91:233–352.

Thomas, O., 1888. "Catalogue of the Marsupialia and Monotremata in the collection of the British Museum (Natural History)". British Museum (Natural History): London.

Troughton, E. Le. G., 1967. "Furred animals of Australia". Angus and Robertson: Sydney.

Tyler, M.J. (ed.), 1979. "The status of endangered Australasian wildlife". Royal Zoological Society of South Australia: Adelaide.

Tyndale-Biscoe, H., 1973. "Life of marsupials". Edward Arnold: London.

Whitley, G.P., 1971. "Kangaroos and men". Part 1 of volume 16 of *The Australian Zoologist*.

Ziegler, A.C., 1983. An ecological check-list of New Guinea Recent mammals. Pp 862–92 in "Biogeography and ecology in New Guinea" ed by J.L. Gressitt. Dlr Junk: The Hague.

REFERENCES ABOUT KANGAROOS IN PARTICULAR AREAS

A. For Western Australia.

There is no general modern work specifically for this state. However, the publications of the Western Australian Wildlife Research Centre of the Department of Fisheries and Wildlife and those of the Western Australian Museum contain excellent survey reports and studies of particular groups of mammals.

B. For South Australia.

Finlayson, H.H., 1961 On central Australian mammals. Part IV. The distribution and status of central Australian species. *Rec. S. Aust. Mus.* 14:141-91.

Jones, F.W., 1924. "The mammals of South Australia. Part II. Containing the bandicoots and the herbivorous marsupials". Government Printer: Adelaide.

Twidale, C.R., Tyler, M.J. and Webb, B.P. (eds), 1976. "Natural history of the Adelaide Region". Royal Society of South Australia: Adelaide.

C. For the Northern Territory.

Frith, H.J. and Calaby, J.H. (eds), 1974. Fauna survey of the Port Essington District, Coburg Peninsula, Northern Territory of Australia. *C.S.I.R.O. Div. of Wildl. Res. Techn. Pap.* No. 28:1–208

Johnson, D.H., 1964. Mammals of the Arnhem Land Expedition. Pp 427–515 *in* "Records of the American-Australian Scientific Expedition to Arnhem Land, Vol. 4 (Zoology)" ed by R.L. Specht. Melbourne University Press: Melbourne.

Parker, S., 1973. An annotated checklist of the native land mammals of the Northern Territory. *Rec. S. Aust. Mus.* 16:1–57.

D. For Queensland.

Breeden, S. and Breeden, K., 1970. "Tropical Queensland". William Collins (Australia) Ltd: Hong Kong.

Davies, W. (ed.), 1983. "Wildlife of the Brisbane area". Jacaranda Press: Milton.

Lavery, H.J. (ed.), 1978. "Exploration north". Richmond Hill Press: Richmond.

Tate, G.H.H., 1952. Results of the Archbold Expeditions. No. 66. Mammals of Cape York Peninsula, with notes on the occurrence of rain forest in Queensland. *Bull. Amer. Mus. Nat. Hist.* 98:563–616.

E. For New South Wales.

Calaby, J.H., 1966. Mammals of the Upper Richmond and Clarence Rivers, New South Wales. *Tech. Pap. Div. Wildl. Surv. C.S.I.R.O. Aust.* No. 10:1–55.

Haigh, C. (ed), 1980. "Kangaroos and other macropods of New South Wales". New South Wales National Parks and Wildlife Service: Sydney.

Marlow, B.J., 1958. A survey of the marsupials of New South Wales. *Wildl. Res.* 3:71–114.

F. For Victoria.

Brazenor, C.W., 1950. "The mammals of Victoria". Brown, Prior and Anderson: Melbourne.

Hampton, J.W.F., Howard, A.E., Poynton, J. and Barnett, J.L., 1982. Records of the mammal survey group of Victoria, 1966–80, on the distribution of terrestrial mammals in Victoria. *Aust. Wildl. Res.* 9:177–201.

Seebeck, J.H., 1977. Mammals in the Melbourne metropolitan area. *Vict. Nat.* 94:165–71.

G. For Tasmania.

Green, R.H., 1973. "The mammals of Tasmania". Foot and Playsted: Launceston.

Hope, J.J., 1973. Mammals of the Bass Strait Islands. *Proc. R. Soc. Vic.* 85:163–96.

Sharland, M. 1961. "Tasmanian wild life". Melbourne University Press: Melbourne.

H. For New Guinea.

There is no general work (ancient *or* modern) on New Guinean mammals. On the other hand, there are many publications dealing with specific areas or taxonomic groups that have been published by the American Museum of Natural History (the Bulletins and Novitates of the Archbold Expeditions) and British Museum of Natural History. The most up-to-date (but out of date) annotated checklist is Laurie and Hill:

Laurie, E.M.O. and Hill, J.E., 1954. "List of land mammals of New Guinea, Celebes and adjacent islands 1758–1952". British Museum (Natural History): London.

THE KANGAROO AND THE FUTURE

ABITAT CHANGES and the introduction of so many exotic species, now feral, have had far-reaching effects on Australia's macropods. Some have benefited from increased grasslands and water that have accompanied pastoral activities. Some have suffered severe reductions in range. Some have become extinct. Logic suggests that the conservation of the remaining species will be best secured by careful habitat management, thoughtful allocation of suitable reserves and control of feral animals. The main public focus on macropod conservation is, however, not on those issues at all, and not on the animals which need it most. Instead, the public focus is almost entirely on the large kangaroos, which are not endangered, and on the kangaroo industry. It is often claimed that the harvest threatens the survival of the large kangaroos, and the kangaroo debate has become a controversial issue in Australia and overseas. This chapter will try to review the complexities of this difficult issue, which is undoubtedly the dominant single wildlife issue in Australia.

The kangaroo, inevitably, has become the symbol of Australia and it is no wonder that the commercial harvesting of these beautiful creatures has become an emotionally charged issue. Yet kangaroos have been harvested for meat and leather for more than a century and in the 65 years for which records are available an average of more than a million skins has been exported annually, mostly those of Red, Eastern Grey and Western Grey Kangaroos. The kangaroo industry grew out of the recognition that kangaroo leather is of especially high strength and quality. It is used particularly for shoes, as well as belts, handbags, wallets and children's toys. Meat is often a profitable sideline. Fears about the diminution of populations as a result of harvesting have been expressed continually by many people, and Australians collectively would undoubtedly agree that no economic return would justify that risk. However, the harvesting and conservation issue is not in any way simple, because many species of kangaroos and wallabies are, or are perceived to be agricultural and pastoral pests. Government policy tries to direct the harvesting towards cropping these, in a pest control role.

Arguments against the industry which are based on fears about extinction or severe diminution of the populations of large kangaroos may be dubbed "numerical" arguments. However, most people now accept that the populations of Reds and Eastern and Western Greys are able to sustain a variable and regulated harvest. There remains, nevertheless, a great deal of opposition on the basis of cruelty, animal rights and, particularly, an argument which calls into question the morality of commercial exploitation of wildlife. These "ethical" arguments, which will be reviewed later, are the arena into which the debate has now moved.

PERCEPTION AND STATUS OF MACROPODS AS A GROUP

Talk of "kangaroos" all too frequently lumps at least several species together; usually the term covers the large commercial species and that is the context in which the term has been used in the introduction to this chapter. This ignores most of the species in the super-family, and all of the animals whose status is threatened. Among the Macropodoidea, most Australians are probably familiar only with the large Red and Grey Kangaroo and might know in a vague way that there are also several types of wallabies, which are smaller than kangaroos, and euros (or wallaroos) which are shaggier looking and intermediate in size. Of the diversity of species in these gneral categories and the other macropods such as bettongs and potoroos, most Australians are probably largely unaware.

The conservation status of the macropods as a whole presents a very bleak picture by comparison with the way things are thought to have been at the time of white settlement. Of 49 recognised Australian species in the Macropodoidea, 5 are presumed extinct and a further 23 are known or thought to have declined since European settlement. Hunting is thought to have contributed to the extinction of the Toolache Wallaby (*Macropus greyi*). For the most part, however, habitat changes and the introduction of exotic animals which became feral have been, and continue to be, the main causes underlying reductions in range and numbers. In contrast, 10 species are likely to have benefited from habitat changes occurring since European settlement, and it is mostly these species which figure in commerce and/or pest control: they are mainly the large kangaroos. Several of the smaller species also figure in the commercial harvest and it is unfortunate that the data base backing up the safety of this practice is not as adequate or as easy to come by as it is for the large species to which aerial survey is applicable.

GREY KANGAROOS NUZZLING.

It is fortuitous that there are so many island refuges which have protected many of the smaller macropods while the mainland populations failed in the face of habitat change and predation. Without the island remnants, the list of extinct species would be much longer. Whereas we may all now lament that insufficient habitat was left, either deliberately or accidentally, in the right places to have prevented the extinctions that have occurred, we can also urge for intelligent habitat reservation from now on. As far as legal protection is concerned, nowhere in Australia can any macropod be killed or captured legally, except by Aborigines, unless a permit is obtained. (There are two exceptions: in the north of the Northern Territory – Agile Wallabies – and in Western Australia where an an open season is sometimes declared locally on Grey Kangaroos.) Undoubtedly, however, considering the vastness of the country and the small number of wildlife rangers, many are shot illegally, either for (unauthorised) pest control, sport or to obtain food for sheep dogs or cattle dogs. It is probable that illegal killing focuses most on species numerous enough to be seen as pests by farmers or graziers. Luckily many of the threatened species occur away from farmlands, often in inaccessible country, so they are less likely to be mistaken for pest species.

NUMBERS AND THE LARGE KANGAROOS

For many species the information about their present status is the result of an educated guess rather than being based on the sort of solid information that we would like to have. The dearth of solid numerical information about many of the species is not surprising, there being no easy way to count many of the smaller wallabies, potoroos, etc., most of which live in brush or amongst rocks and in rough country. The large kangaroos, which comprise most of the commercial harvest, provide a sharp contrast because of their distribution and an index of population density can be achieved relatively simply and cheaply over wide areas by aerial survey. Particularly over the past 10–12 years there has been extensive application of this method, developed mainly by Dr Graeme Caughley at CSIRO Wildlife and Rangelands Research in Canberra.

In practice, the survey method is simple. A small, high-wing four or six seat aircraft is flown at 76 m above ground level along a series

THE KANGAROO ISLAND KANGAROO...FEARLESS IN ITS ISLAND HOME.

IS THE FUTURE ONE VAST EMPTY PLAIN?

of predetermined flight lines within a particular survey block. A trained observer on each side of the aircraft scans a 200 metre wide strip of ground as it slides by his window, the outer edge being marked by a cord streaming back from the wing strut. At 100 knots it takes 97 seconds to cover 5 km, by which time each observer will have scanned 1 sq km of ground, counting any kangaroos seen. A buzzer sounds for seven seconds at the end of each unit, giving the observers time to mark their data sheets with the numbers of Reds and Greys seen, if any. Then the next unit is scanned, and the survey proceeds unit by unit, line by line until the end of the session.

Subsequently, these raw data are scaled up in proportion to the total area of the block in question and by a correction factor for sightability. The correction factor allows what would otherwise be an index of density to be scaled up to an estimate of total numbers, taking into account the fact that not all kangaroos on a scanned strip are seen by the observer. Even in grassland a trained observer will miss at least half the animals, and more in heavily timbered country. Accordingly, there are habitat-related correction factors by which the raw counts are multiplied to obtain an estimate of the total number of animals in the survey area. It is becoming clear that the correction factors are fairly good for Reds but probably too low for Greys, so that the corrections used up to now underestimate real numbers of Greys. This matters little; underestimates are on the safe side, and the discrepancy does not detract from the value of the method in tracking population trends.

There is quite a learning process in developing a search image for Reds and Greys, and learning to reject Euros which are normally not counted. It also takes time to learn to work, relaxed and happy, in a noisy, often hot and bumpy aircraft. It seems to take a new observer about 50 hours to learn to cope with the discomfort, maintain the required steady and high level of concentration, and identify, sort and store separately the images he identifies as Red or Grey Kangaroos. To train an observer, we put him or her on the same side as an experienced observer so they scan the same strip. At the beginning, the novice may see something like 50 per cent or less of the trained observer's score. This gradually improves and a "learning curve" is plotted to establish when performance has stabilised. This takes many sessions. Luckily, most people seem to show similar

THE RED KANGAROO: THE BASIS OF THE KANGAROO SHOOTING INDUSTRY.

A JOEY PEEPS OUT TO NIBBLE ON THE GREEN GRASS.

skills, but a separate correction factor can be made for any observer with a notably different performance. Not surprisingly, some people prove unsuitable; observing is a very demanding task and requires a high level of concentration and dedication.

Regular aerial surveys of the three large kangaroos are undertaken at present by a University of Sydney team in the South Australian Pastoral Zone (since 1978) and by a New South Wales National Parks and Wildlife Service team in New South Wales west of the Great Dividing Range (since 1975–76). Although this represents only a small part of the total range of these three species, the animals are most dense in the sheep-growing regions, with New South Wales and South Australia having about 70% of all Western Greys, 50% of Reds and (more approximately) 25% of Eastern Greys. Surveys in these areas were supplemented by a series of 'the rest of Australia' surveys in the period 1980–82, undertaken by Graeme Caughley and CSIRO, so that in 1983 estimates for the whole country could be calculated for the first time. Total estimates were 8.4 million Reds, 1.8 million Western Greys and 9 million Eastern Greys. As a result of a series of good breeding seasons in the eastern states, populations during the survey period were probably higher than the long term average. For Greys though, the result is almost certainly an underestimate of what the populations then were, due to the use of conservative correction factors. However, an exact determination of the number of kangaroos is an impossible task. What is needed is a precise index of population density which can be used to monitor trends and to identify the significant factors affecting the dynamics of the populations. Aerial survey provides a useful way to achieve this. In South Australia and New South Wales, results from the annual surveys contribute to the decision about what harvesting quotas to recommend in these States for the following year. Quotas are set by the Australian National Parks and Wildlife Service, taking into account survey data and other information from all the States.

As a result of the repetitive standardised surveys in South Australia and New South Wales particularly, combined with the results from the first all-Australian survey and other data, some conclusions can be drawn which are relevant to the question of the status of the three large species, their conservation and management:

All three species are abundant and widespread. They are most numerous in the pastoral regions, within the dingo-proof fences, coinciding with Australia's sheep country. This is probably partly because sheep and kangaroos appear to have similar climatic preferences and partly because the provision of more watering points and pasture management inside the dog fences benefits kangaroos as well as sheep. Outside the fence there is likely to be more predation by dingos. However, the effects of the dog fences and pastoral management on kangaroo demography are not yet fully understood.

Assessing trends in South Australia and New South Wales over the past seven years or more, it is clear that there may be enormous short term fluctuations in numbers and, furthermore, that these fluctuations are driven mainly by the opposing forces of rainfall and drought. Widespread rainfall provides grass, the preferred feed, which then leads to large and rapid population increases. In good conditions an annual rate of increase of at least 25 per cent can be maintained. Drought may cause precipitous falls in density, depending on its severity. An example of this can be seen in South Australia where the recent drought, said by many to be one of the worst on record, led in 1983 to a fall in Western Greys to 56 per cent and Reds to 62 per cent of 1982 numbers. In New South Wales falls to 55 per cent and 59 per cent were recorded in a similar period, almost identical in both states. Such wide fluctuations are completely different from what is seen in human populations, which may account for many of the fears about kangaroos. The idea of a population losing 40–50 per cent (or even more) of its members may fill an observer with horror but the reality is that kangaroos have been coping with drought for millenia and a population reduced by severe drought is able to increase rapidly when conditions improve.

The data give no indication that the legal plus illegal shooting of kangaroos makes much impact on kangaroo densities. Although common sense dictates that pest control in a localised area can cause a local decline, this appears to be quite lost in the overall picture. In a run of good seasons from 1978–81, numbers throughout most of South Australia increased continuously despite annual legal harvests of 100–200,000 animals (6–9 per cent of the populations over those years) and an unknown illegal kill. There seems also to be a built-in, density-related control over the number taken by the industry, quite

A WESTERN GREY KANGAROO, THE MOST ABUNDANT LARGE MACROPOD IN AUSTRALIA'S SOUTHWEST.

A PLAYFUL BABY RED-NECKED WALLABY.

separate from any control by management authorities, because kangaroo shooting is so far economic only when and where kangaroos are abundant.

Agricultural and pastoral industries have rather different consequences for the large kangaroos. Whereas the pastoral industry has undoubtedly had a severely deleterious effect on many of the macropods, it is likely that the large kangaroos have benefited from it. In contrast, wheat farming areas carry only very low densities of kangaroos, and wherever wheat and kangaroos come into conflict kangaroos seem to lose out.

In short, none of the three large kangaroos is endangered and arguments against the regulated commercial industry cannot continue to be based upon claims that the industry threatens kangaroos with extinction. If arguments against the industry are to be made, they must be made on other grounds.

ETHICAL CONSIDERATIONS

Whereas aerial surveys and other information have reinforced the view that controlled commercial exploitation of kangaroos will not pose a threat, questions about the morality of having such an industry are another matter. With the "numerical" arguments out of the way, the "ethical" ones remain. Ultimately, it must be a well-informed community which makes the decision and a crucial factor may be the results of work now in progress to assess the extent to which kangaroos really are pests to farmers and graziers when the numbers are high. That assertion has yet to come under really close scrutiny for, though local competition between sheep and cattle in times of drought has been demonstrated, more information is needed about the quantitative impact of this. At present, government policy accepts that several species of kangaroos and wallabies are a significant pest in high numbers, and the commerical industry is therefore a self-supporting "tool of management" for pest reduction. In this way, the essential issue is avoided, of whether or not the value of the resource itself provides sufficient justification for its exploitation. The government policy of justifying the industry because of its pest control role is not accepted everywhere. The Australian Conservation Foundation and the Kangaroo Protection Committee both accept that pest control measures are sometimes necessary. However, both these organisations oppose the making of any commercial gain from this, advocating instead that government shooters should do the work as required, leaving the carcasses unused. The cost of this is a strong argument usually put forward against this proposal, and the idea of kangaroo shooter public servants, with overtime, wet-weather money and working to rules is no more appealing than the likely alternative of paying a bounty on pairs of ears or a tail. Interestingly, the opposition to accepting a commercial value for wildlife seems to be counter to what is increasingly being referred to in Australia and overseas as "value-added conservation"; the idea that a dollar value promotes the conservation of the resource, with some of the money from the sale of the resource being fed back towards research, monitoring and management by government agencies.

One of the fears expressed frequently is that, in setting harvest quotas, National Parks and Wildlife Service organisations will listen more to the kangaroo industry than to the needs of damage mitigation or kangaroo conservation. However, one argument against this is that government quotas are seldom reached, so the main factor controlling the number of kangaroos taken is the economics of seek, shoot, and sell, there being money to be made only when the animals are numerous, in the present market circumstances.

The urging of non-government organisations and private individuals has obviously played a very important role in shaping the present policies towards kangaroos and to the industry, and I have no doubt that there is lot more urging ahead. Wildlife authorities, with the responsibility for ensuring the safety of the fauna, sit in the middle, trying to steer some rational course between farmers and graziers who would like to see big reductions in numbers, and many conservation groups who would like to see the end of all shooting.

But not all conservation bodies have similar views. Both the Nature Conservation Society of South Australia and the Royal Zoological Society of New South Wales accept the idea of utilising kangaroos as a renewable resource and neither organisation sees the necessity to look elsewhere than the value of the resource itself to provide a justification. On the other hand, animal liberation groups oppose killing kangaroos, and all other animals. The view, however,

THE COMMERCIALLY HARVESTED EASTERN GREY KANGAROO, SAFE IN THE SNOW.

that would seek to prohibit commercial harvesting just simply because kangaroos are wildlife is seen by many to be philosophically illogical because the distinction between wildlife and domestic animals is a human invention. Certainly it is difficult to see by what logic we should condone killing individual cattle and sheep, yet reject the idea of killing individual kangaroos. Likely there is little difference from the perspective of the victims. How much value can we put on the common argument that excuses killing domesticated animals because they were bred for the purpose, yet condemns killing a kangaroo? Are we to believe that cattle and sheep have agreed to some sort of bargain with humans in which they ultimately pay for their board and keep with their carcass? Interestingly, animal welfare organisations are continually urging the community in favour of free-range animal management rather than intensive animal production units with their poor quality lifestyle for pigs, hens, cattle and so on. Yet many of the same organisations deplore the commercial harvesting of free-range kangaroos, which live their whole lives as free beings until the shooter comes along and, in the case of a small proportion of the population, ends it in a split second.

CONCLUSION

So the scientific understanding and information lead to the conclusion that, unlike whales and many other species of animals, the large kangaroos really can sustain a regulated commercial industry. Furthermore, rational and logical considerations lead to the conclusion that the humane utilisation of kangaroos as a renewable resource is not immoral. The former conclusion is established beyond doubt; the latter is a philosophical viewpoint. Whatever one's philosophy, however, there is no simple solution.

Some of the best words I have heard on the kangaroo issue came from Peter Ellyard at the evening session of the June 1983 Public Forum on Kangaroo Management held in Adelaide and I quote them here, (with some minor editing) letting him have the last word:

> "I stand before you today speaking, as I said, personally, as a committed vegetarian. I don't condone the killing of kangaroos or of anything else for that matter. . . .

RED KANGAROOS SEEK SHADE UNDER A SPARSE DESERT TREE.

"... what should be our attitude to the harvesting of wildlife? I don't personally see any great difference between killing a cow or a kangaroo, or for that matter a harp seal pup. I recognise that many people see a huge difference and I think they should ask themselves why they feel this difference. What values lie behind such a view? It is clear that what people regard as acceptable to kill and eat depends a lot on culture. Hindus don't kill cows but eat pork. Moslems don't kill pigs but eat beef. . . .

"Kangaroos are also, of course, a symbol of our nation and I think it is worthwhile asking whether this status means that we should treat kangaroos differently from other animals; whether this anthropocentric elevation of the kangaroo really should make any difference.

"If we are honest we have to admit that our values about killing wildlife are culturally based, sometimes religious (but this is not the case with kangaroos), changing and arbitrary. However, are there fundamental issues that should be considered in determining our attitude to the taking of wildlife? Clearly there are.

"First, we clearly should not kill fauna if, by doing so, we endanger the species. Therefore this should determine our attitude to whales and crocodiles which most people would not think of as being particularly lovely. Kangaroos clearly are lovely but are also, clearly, not endangered. Kangaroos have reproductive systems that allow them to recover their population after decline due to drought, or any other factors, faster than placental mammals.

"Second, we should also consider the conservation status of the environment in which the fauna lives. Kangaroos live widely in the rangelands of arid and semi-arid Australia. Much of this rangeland has been significantly degraded by the pastoral industry based on sheep and cattle, and considerable desertification has resulted and is continuing. The major cause of this is the sheep and cattle industry. I believe it is imperative for the long term viability of this ecosystem that large parts of arid and semi-arid Australia should be closed down to cattle and sheep. Kangaroos clearly do not endanger this ecosystem, after all they evolved there. It is worth considering whether or not we should actively *encourage* the development of a viable kangaroo industry

WALLABIES SUCH AS THIS GENERALLY ESCAPE THE COMMERCIALISM.

in order to create the economic opportunity to get sheep and cattle out of this rangeland country. I believe it is likely that if we set up a well-organised kangaroo industry based on the promotion of meat for human consumption, rather than pet food, as an economic alternative to sheep and cattle in this country, it would be feasible. The conservation benefits to Australian rangelands would be enormous and, in my view, most worthwhile.

"A third matter worth considering is an issue which is of concern to animal liberationists. A lot of emotional energy is invested in kangaroo killing methods. Clearly there is great room for improvement but despite this I believe that a bullet through the head on the range is preferable to the final days spent by the average sheep or cow in the abattoir. This issue does not get the attention it deserves.

"Conservationists often portray the kangaroo industry as greedy and callous. . . . This sort of killing is brutal, but no more brutal than the acts performed daily in the abattoir, which are condoned by the actions of all people, including conservationists, who eat meat.

"Conservationists do not help their cause by their posturing that they are the occupiers of the moral high ground and that their opponents are greedy brutes. Let us have dialogue. No matter how many kangaroos are killed, some conservationists will say too many are being killed. How many is enough – 5 per cent, 10 per cent, 15 per cent of total population killed per annum? The bargaining should be about what percentage should be harvested. Let us agree on what percentage is a reasonable one and let a programme of harvesting then proceed, concentrating on minimising the violence and agony suffered by the kangaroo, and without the moral posturing and emotional hysteria.

"Let us then consider in a more thorough way the issues (moral, economic, social, ecological) which are involved in this debate and divorce it from the debate about populations and percentages to be harvested. Let us consider all these issues involved and see if we can make some progress. Unless we really try to be reasonable, we will make as little progress in the next decade as we have in the last."

AN EARLY EUROPEAN RENDITION OF THE AUSTRALIAN KANGAROO.

TABLE OF KANGAROO SPECIES SHOWING THEIR CONSERVATION STATUS AND CHANGE SINCE EUROPEAN SETTLEMENT

SCIENTIFIC NAME	COMMON NAME	STATUS	PEST DESTRUCTION SOMETIMES?	COMMERCIAL USE?	CHANGE SINCE SETTLEMENT	LIKELY REASON
FAMILY POTOROIDAE (POTOROOS, BETTONGS AND RAT-KANGAROOS)						
Hypsiprymnodon moschatus	Musky Rat-kangaroo	Common, limited vulnerable	—	—	Range reduced	Rainforest clearing in North Qld.
Potorous tridactylus	Long-nosed Potoroo	Common, limited	—	—	Range reduced	Clearing of east coast forests
Potorous platyops	Broad-faced Potoroo	Extinct	—	—	Extinction	Unknown.
Potorous longipes	Long-footed Potoroo	Rare, endangered	—	—	Unknown	Habitat possibly threatened by wood-chipping
Bettongia penicillata	Brush-tailed Bettong	Rare, endangered	—	—	Range reduced severely	Land clearing & impact of grazing animals
Bettongia tropica	Tropical Bettong	Limited, vulnerable	—	—	Range reduced	
Bettongia gaimardi	Tasmanian Bettong	Common	—	—	Extinct on mainland Common in Tasmania	Fox predation, habitat changes
Bettongia lesueur	Burrowing Bettong	Limited, vulnerable (WA islands)	—	—	Extinct on mainland	Rabbits, foxes, cats
Aepyprymnus rufescens	Rufous Bettong (or Rat-kangaroo)	Common	—	—	Range reduced	Land clearing, grazing
Caloprymnus campestris	Desert Rat-kangaroo	Presumed extinct	—	—	Extinction?	Unknown
FAMILY MACROPODIDAE (KANGAROOS AND WALLABIES)						
HARE WALLABIES						
Lagorchestes leporides	Eastern Hare-wallaby	Extinct	—	—	Extinction	Grazing
Lagorchestes conspicillatus	Spectacled Hare-wallaby	Common (Qld) elsewhere rare, abundant Barrow Is.	—	—	Decline on mainland	Grazing
Lagorchestes hirsutus	Rufous Hare-wallaby	Rare, vulnerable	—	—	Range severely reduced	Changed wildfire regime
Lagorchestes asomatus	Central Hare-wallaby	Extinct	—	—	Extinct	
Lagostrophus fasciatus	Banded Hare-wallaby	Vulnerable, limited to two WA islands	—	—	Extinct on mainland	
NAILTAIL WALLABIES						
Onychogalea unguifera	Northern Nailtail	Common	—	—	Local reductions in numbers	Little known
Onychogalea fraenata	Bridled Nailtail	Endangered	—	—	Range severely reduced	Pastoral industry
Onychogalea lunata	Crescent Nailtail	Presumed extinct	—	—	Decline to extinction	Agriculture in NSW?
ROCK WALLABIES						
Petrogale lateralis	Black-footed Rock Wallaby	Vulnerable, scattered	—	—	Range reduction	Foxes
Petrogale penicillata	Brush-tailed Rock Wallaby	Common	—	—	Range reduction	Foxes
Petrogale inornata	Unadorned Rock Wallaby	Common	—	—	Unknown	
etrogale godmani	Godman's Rock Wallaby	Vulnerable	—	—	Unknown	
Petrogale rothschildi	Rothschild's Rock Wallaby	Common, limited	—	—	Unknown	
Petrogale xanthopus	Yellow-footed Rock Wallaby	Vulnerable, limited	—	—	Range severely reduced	Land clearing, goats, grazing
Petrogale persephone	Proserpine Rock Wallaby	Rare, endangered	—	—	Unknown	May be threatened by "natural" circumstances
Petrogale brachyotis	Short-eared Rock Wallaby	Common	—	—	Probably little change	
Petrogale burbidgei	Warabi	Common, limited	—	—	Little or none	
Petrogale concinna	Narbarlek, Little Rock Wallaby	Vulnerable, limited	—	—	Little or none	

SCIENTIFIC NAME	COMMON NAME	STATUS	PEST DESTRUCTION SOMETIMES?	COMMERCIAL USE?	CHANGE SINCE SETTLEMENT	LIKELY REASON
PADEMELONS						
Thylogale stigmatica	Red-legged Pademelon	Common	—	—	Range reduction	Clearing of rainforest
Thylogale billiardierii	Tasmanian Pademelon	Abundant	Yes	Yes	Extinct on Mainland	Unknown
					Prob. increase in Tasmania	Clearing for agriculture adjacent to forest
Thylogale thetis	Red-necked Pademelon	Common	Yes (but not legally)	No	Local eruptions	Clearing for agriculture adjacent to forest
TYPICAL WALLABIES AND KANGAROOS						
Macropus parma	Parma Wallaby	Secure, scattered	—	—	Range reduction	Vulnerable to forest clearing
Macropus eugenii	Tammar Wallaby	Common, limited	Sometimes on Kangaroo Is.	—	Range severely reduced	Land clearing for wheat, cats
Macropus greyi	Toolache Wallaby	Extinct	—	—	Extinction	Hunting, foxes, Used for coursing
Macropus irma	Western Brush Wallaby	Common	—	—	Population decline	Land clearing, foxes
Macropus parryi	Whiptail Wallaby	Common	Yes	Yes (Qld)	Local eruptions	Grazer, benefited from grassland increase
Macropus dorsalis	Black-striped Wallaby	Common	Yes (Qld)	Yes (Qld)	Range reduction, but local eruptions (Qld)	Agriculture, grazing
Macropus rufogriseus	Red-necked or Bennett's Wallaby	Common	Yes	Yes (Tas & Qld)	Little change, local eruptions	Agriculture
Macropus agilis	Agile Wallaby	Abundant	Yes (Qld)	No	Little change or increase	Pastoral industry
Macropus gigantus	Eastern Grey Kangaroo	Abundant	Yes	Yes	Increase	Pastoral industry
Macropus fuliginosus	Western Grey Kangaroo	Abundant	Yes	Yes	Increase	Pastoral industry
Macropus robustus	Common Wallaroo	Abundant	Yes	Yes	Little change or increase	Pastoral industry
Macropus antilopinus	Antilopine Wallaroo	Common	—	—	Little change or increase	Pastoral industry
Macropus bernardus	Black Wallaroo	Vulnerable, restricted	—	—	Little change	
Macropus rufus	Red Kangaroo	Abundant	Yes	Yes	Increase	Pastoral industry
ANOMALOUS WALLABIES						
Setonix Brachyurus	Quokka	Vulnerable, limited	—	—	Range reduced	
Wallabia bicolor	Swamp Wallaby	Common	Yes (Qld)	Yes (Qld)	Little change local eruptions	
TREE KANGAROOS						
Dendrolagus lumholtzi	Lumholtz's Tree-kangaroo	Vulnerable, limited	—	—	Range severely reduced	Clearing of rainforests
Dendrolagus bennetianus	Bennett's Tree-kangaroo	Vulnerable, limited	—	—	Range reduced	Clearing of rainforests
NEW GUINEA KANGAROOS						
Dorcopsulus vanheurni	Little Dorcopsis	Common	No	No	Little change	
Dorcopsulus macleayi	Macleay's Dorcopsis	Vulnerable	No	No	Unknown	May be threatened by "natural" circumstances
Dorcopsis hageni	White-striped Dorcopsis	Common	No	No	Little change	
Dorcopsis luctuosa	Grey Dorcopsis	Common	No	No	Little change	
Dorcopsis veterum	Brown Dorcopsis	Common	No	No	Little change	
Dorcopsis atrata	Black Dorcopsis	Vulnerable	No	No	Unknown	Restricted habitat, hunting?
Thylogale braunii	Dusky Pademelon	Common	No	No	Little change	
Thylogale christenseni	Christensen's Thylogale	Extinct?	No	No	Unknown	
Dendrolagus dorianus	Doria's Tree-kangaroo	Vulnerable	No	No	Some range reduction	Hunting
Dendrolagus goodfellowi	Goodfellow's Tree-kangaroo	Vulnerable	No	No	Unknown	Hunting
Dendrolagus inustus	Grizzled Tree-kangaroo	Vulnerable	No	No	Unknown	Hunting
Dendrolagus ursinus	Vogelkop Tree-kangaroo	Vulnerable	No	No	Unknown	Hunting
Dendrolagus matschiei	Matschie's Tree-kangaroo	Vulnerable	No	No	Unknown	Hunting

This table has been assembled from many published sources with assistance from Jan Grigg to whom we are grateful as well as to John Calaby who ran his expert eye over it and made invaluable suggestions.

END NOTES

The three superb illustrations for Chapter One were drawn especially for this edition by Sydney artist Rod Scott. They appear on Pp 19,23,27.
Rod Scott's previous commissions include two major Australian works, Furred and Feathered Friends, and Wildlife Heritage. As well he has done a number of major overseas commissions. He specialises in wildlife for which he has a great love. He is regarded as one of Australia's leading such illustrators. On Pp 32,55,112,232 an illustration provided by the Mitchell Library in Sydney has been repeated. On Pp 118,132,140,146,188 and 255 the work of the 19th century naturalist Gould has been used.

The major photographic work was shot by Sydney nature photographer Leo Meier and Canberra wildlife photographer Jean-Paul Ferrero. Their work appears as follows:

Jean-Paul Ferrero: Pp 2,3,5,6,7,8,12,13,14,16,35,36,41,43,45,47,48,51,53,54, 57,60,61,62,67,69,70,71,74,75,78,79,82,84,85,86,88,93,95,99,103,104,107, 116,138,142,154,158,160,174,180,182,184,186,190,192,194,196,198,200, 202,206,208,210,212,214,237,245,246,249,251.

Leo Meier: Pp 1,29,37,38,64,65,72,73,76,77,80,81,83,87,90,91,92,96,101, 109,110,115,130,140,156,235,238,239,241,242,253.

Other work was provided by photographers whose work is on file at the National Photographic Index of Australian Wildlife. They were:

J.B. Cooper: 120, H. and J. Beste: 122, A.G. Wells: 124,126,170, R.H. Green: 128, J. and P. Gardner: 130, Graham Robertson: 136, P.M. Johnson: 150, L.J. Roberts: 152, Kim White: 162, J. and D. Bartlett: 164, G.D. Sanson: 166, R. Close: 172, G.B. Baker: 176, B.G. Thomson: 178.

Also contributing was Philip Quirk: p.140 (inset).

INDEX

*Alphabetical arrangement is letter-by-letter. Italic
numerals refer to an illustration; those in bold type indicate
the main body of information on a subject.*